Praise for *Daring to Dream Once Again*

"Dinah has lived a fascinating and unconventional life. She has done all the things that make life rich and fulfilling: raising a family, building a career, living abroad, and finding one's roots, but she has done them out of order, sometimes swept by life's tides, sometimes driven by her own dreams.

She does everything with passion and devotion and has lived every stage of her life to the fullest. Her courage to follow her dreams and her grit and grace when faced with adversity are evident in this book. This extraordinary life story, told with clarity and candor, is truly inspirational."

Victoria Zhang, Ph.D., co-author of *The Road to Princeton: The Wisdom of Raising Dan Li* and Director, SAP Labs

"Dinah is an absolute treasure. Full of wisdom and insight, her words will inspire you to be true to your Inner Wisdom no matter what."

Amy Ahlers, bestselling author of *Reform Your Inner Mean Girl* and *Big Fat Lies Women Tell Themselves*

"I'd recommend Dinah Lin's memoir as a fascinating read for all women. For the older generation, to understand the tough battles she fought and won all on her own in the male-dominated political and business worlds. For today's generation of women, benefiting from those like Dinah clearing the paths for them, as an inspiration to reach for their own dreams. A must-read for any Women Studies course."

Ann Bridges, author of *Private Offerings* and former Silicon Valley executive

"Inspiring, warm-hearted and true, Dinah's story is a wonderful gift to the world."

Sam Bennett, author of *Get It Done: From Procrastination to Creative Genius in 15 Minutes a Day*

"Dinah Lin's book is an inspiring and transformational example of how one's clarity, empowering beliefs, and plan of action can turn dreams into reality. Her story shows that you can achieve whatever you want, at any age, regardless of your circumstances. It all begins with a dream. Dinah uses her own culture, family traditions, and challenges to share the lessons of her life and to support us in making our own dreams come true.

I congratulate Dinah on being living proof that it's never too late."

Maggie Schreiber, Certified Dream Coach® and Founder of Women Of Wonder

Daring to Dream Once Again

A Memoir

Daring to Dream Once Again

It's Never Too Late!

DINAH LIN

Transformation Books Publishing
York, Pennsylvania

DARING TO DREAM ONCE AGAIN
It's Never Too Late

Copyright© 2015 by Dinah Lin

All rights reserved. No part of this book may be reproduced or transmitted in any form or by any means, electronic or mechanical, including photography, recording or in any information storage or retrieval system without written permission from the author and publisher.

Cover design by: Dinah Lin and Ranilo Cabo
Editor: Steven Bauer
Author photograph: Lisa DeNeffe

Published by:
Transformation Books
211 Pauline Drive #513
York, PA 17402
www.TransformationBooks.com

ISBN: 978-0-9862901-4-5
Library of Congress Control Number: 2015943616

Printed in the United States of America

To my beloved mother, Jean C. Lin, whose courage,
determination and dream brought us to America.
She understood me better than anyone,
and I miss her more than words can tell.

To my children, Jeffrey and Debbie,
and grandchildren, Nicole, Brandon and Liana,
I cherish the precious memories you've given me
and look forward to many more to come.

And to all who dare to dream.

Contents

Introduction 1

A Mother's Dream 5
   A Privileged Childhood 6
   Escaping Shanghai 10
   "The China Doctor" 13
   Attitude and Adapting 15
   A True Patriot 18

A Daughter's Dream 21
   First Taste of America 22
   Magical First Christmas 23
   Little Green Schoolhouse 24
   Growing Up American 26
   A Touching Insight 28
   Prejudice 30
   A Dream Come True 32

Living Someone Else's Dream 37
    You Did It Backwards! 38
    Five Countries in Fifteen Years 42
    You're Just Too American! 45
    Longing To Do More 46
    A Life Changing Revelation 49

A Dream of My Own 55
    There Has to Be More 56
    Why Do You Want a Job? 58
    Shoe on the Other Foot 61
    A Kris Through My Heart 63
    What Are You Going To Do? 66
    Rip Van Wrinkle 67
    My Overlooked Diamond 69
    They Got Two Points For You! 73
    Presenting to the Executive Committee 78
    Heart Over Head 81
    Resigning On Principle 84
    Losing Dad 86
    "A Kinder, Gentler Nation" 89
    Ignorance Can Be A Blessing 90
    They Hired You On Merit! 98
    Leaving A Legacy 100
    "The Best of Both Worlds" 106
    A Sandwich Not a Buffet 108

It's A Can of Worms!	112
An Unforgettable New Year's Eve	117
Putting China On the Radar Screen	120
McDonald's At Tiananmen Square	123
China Postscript	125
Leaving Corporate America	125

Following A Dream Back Home 129

China 1973	130
Crisis = Wei Ji	134
Down On My Knees	137
Going to Beijing!	138
Xijiao Hotel and Global Village	139
Best Deal in Beijing	141
New Oriental School	142
Which Do You Love More?	145
The SARS Scare	147
Heaven and Earth Change Places	150
Back in the Business World	152
Super 8 With Chandeliers	155
Mutianyu Schoolhouse at the Great Wall	159
Stepping Onto the World Stage	162
Her Spirit Left	168

Daring To Dream Once Again 173

Time to Return Home	174

Close to Dying 177
Rescuing My Dream 177
Returning to Freedom 179
Dark Night of the Soul 181
15 Minutes a Day Magic 184
Transformational Author 186
A Mother's Wish For Her Daughter 190

About the Author 194

Introduction

This book is a dream come true for me, a dream that refused to die. It waited patiently for me, for several decades, until one day it could wait no longer. In 2010, I relocated to the U.S. after spending a decade in Beijing. I went to China after "retirement," to study Chinese and re-connect with my roots. Of course I hadn't planned on staying a decade.

One day, out of nowhere, and seemingly for no reason, I burst into tears while driving, which turned into sobbing. Deep down, I knew why my heart was crying. I was letting my dream of writing a book slip away…day by day, month by month, and year by year. I knew then, with every fiber of my being, that I simply had to write my book, and time was of the essence. I was soon turning 70, and for the first time in my life, I contemplated my remaining days on earth. There was still much I wished to do, to contribute to others, and I needed to start by writing my book.

Sometimes in life we cause ourselves to travel a circuitous route, because we resist what we know deep down. The vision seems too grand, and scares us. I believe all along I knew the story I wished to share was my own story: my pride in being Chinese-American from the time I was a child growing up in Ohio; a life lived on both sides of the globe; doing it "backwards" by starting my career at age 36, obtaining a senior political appointment in Washington, D. C., finally breaking the "glass ceiling" in corporate America and much more. But the idea of writing a memoir seemed pretentious to me. Thus it took me many months and a few false starts before I finally put aside my reservations and simply started writing my stories.

Each person's experience is unique to him or her. At the same time, we are all informed and enriched by each other's experience and stories, living examples of universal truths. By sharing mine, I hope I can remind you of your own precious stories and dreams.

From the outset, I knew I wanted to start with my mom. It was her courage and determination that enabled me, together with my two siblings, to escape on the last boat out of Shanghai before it was taken over by the Communists in 1949. My Dad was already in the U.S. on a one-year research grant, and had planned to return, until Mom wrote him and told him to stay—she'd find a way to get us out.

As I neared the end of writing my stories, I realized each major new phase of my life started with a dream, whether I knew it then or not. Thus the six parts of this book were born, each representing a major new phase of my life.

The title came to me early on, months before I started any writing. I had just come back from a workshop and was using colored pens to free-associate different words. Daring to Dream resonated with me immediately, but the URL was not available. I tried Daring to Dream Once Again and it was available. I liked this even better! A few words, a simple phrase, can shift our emotions and perspective. Daring to dream once again became my challenge to myself, my rallying cry, my inspiration—to finally start writing my book, to know that it's never too late!

It is my fondest hope that this book can be an inspiration to you as well. Believe that it's never too late to make a fresh start, and never too late to dream once again. Whatever your circumstance, whatever stage of life you're at, whatever your age, it's never too late. I like to say, as long as you're breathing it's not too late. Within every soul there's a song waiting to be sung—only you can sing your song your way.

My heartfelt thanks for joining me on my exciting journey. I send you love and blessings as you travel your path, with a dream in your heart.

A Mother's Dream

Freedom lies in being bold
-Robert Frost

A Privileged Childhood

When I was a little girl growing up in Ohio, Mom used to sing Chinese opera. She'd be in the kitchen cooking or elsewhere doing household chores and suddenly break out in a few favorite verses. To my child's ear the high shrills of Peking opera sounded awful, but authentic, like what I'd heard on the radio in Shanghai. I think Mom sang when she was happy, or when she wanted to be happy. It took her back to her childhood days, when she was pampered by her beloved Dad as the youngest child.

I don't know when, or why, Mom stopped her singing, but she did. Maybe it was too hard on the vocal chords. She had learned, as a child, listening to her grandpa who sang as a sideline to help support the family. When we were young both my parents used to share stories of their youth, but with the passing decades, I only remember snippets. Dad died many years before Mom, and I had never thought of taping him. But I had thought of taping Mom, many times, and, never seemed to get around to it.

How is it we let the truly important things and moments in life slip away...while we focus on our 'to do' list?

Thanks to the discovery of a previously unknown cousin living in Beijing and our subsequent conversations, some in Monterey, CA, while she was visiting her daughter, I was able to glean insights into my mom's family I either never knew or had long forgotten.

Mom was the youngest of five children, a decade younger than the next sibling, and nearly twenty years younger than her oldest brother. She was born in Beijing, and always proud of being a 'Beijing person.' The family endured many years of hardship, losing its prosperous trading business during the Boxer Rebellion in the early 1900s. Her grandpa moved the family to Shenyang, the capital of Liaoning Province, northeast of Beijing, to start over again.

Cousin says Mom brought the family good luck. After she was born, the family photography business began to thrive, with elite clients from academia, government, and the film industry.

Her dad regularly traveled to Tokyo to buy special photography films, supplies and equipment. She talked about this in my younger days, but I had forgotten until a happy serendipity occurred.

In the early '90s as Vice President, Worldwide Business Development for Burger King, I regularly traveled to Asia. On one of my business trips back to the U.S. from Beijing connecting through Tokyo, I was wandering around the gift shops in the terminal, looking for something to bring back to Mom. I finally decided to bring her an assortment of Japanese sticky sweet rice balls, hoping she'd like them.

I'd just arrived at Mom's house in Williamsburg, Virginia, after my twenty-four hour (door to door) trip and had not yet unpacked. I came down the stairs into her kitchen, and said, "Mom, I brought a little something back for you; I hope you like it." Opening the box, and seeing what was inside, Mom was like a child at Christmas. With rare emotion she said, "My dad used to always bring these back for me from his trips to Tokyo." I could see a flood of wonderful childhood memories coming back to her as she tasted these sweets. I then remembered her telling me about his trips and always bringing something back for her...I had totally forgotten this! I was so happy I 'happened' to bring her the Japanese sweets this time, and did so each time thereafter.

Being the youngest, and possessed with a sharp and quick mind, she was easily 'Daddy's favorite.' She amused and entertained him when they were together, and her childhood memories were focused on happy times spent with him. Her father died when she was in her early teens, and her oldest brother enrolled her into a nursing school, instead of a four-year university as she had hoped. She once mentioned, and I could hear sadness and regret in her voice, "I believe if my dad had not passed away when he did, he would have allowed me to attend university."

There's a rather romantic story of how Mom and Dad met. The Seventh-Day Adventist church had quite an operation in Shanghai, complete with hospital, clinic, nursing school and more. Dad, a CPA, was the Treasurer for the church's operations. Dad came from a very humble background, and sold textbooks and Bibles to put himself through college. One day he was walking from one building to another, and he spotted Mom playing tennis. Mom was working as a nurse at the hospital. I don't know if it was 'love at first sight' but he took action to meet her. As was the custom then, he needed to have a proper introduction, which he arranged through her oldest brother. Mom was tall, slim and fair skinned in her youth and Dad was a handsome man, together they made an attractive couple. The courtship proceeded smoothly, oldest brother was in favor of the match.

I loved listening to my cousin describe the lavish wedding of my parents, which she had heard recounted by her dad, mom's older brother. Cousin described the abundant array of jade and jewelry that was part of Mom's dowry. I hadn't realized it was the bride's family that gifted the dowry. Cousin said it was to ensure the bride was well treated by the groom's family.

Escaping Shanghai

"Hurry, quick, we can't miss the boat!" There was urgency in my mom's voice and a tinge of fear as she helped us push our way through the mob of people all trying to get on the small ship. We held hands tightly, my younger brother, older sister, and I. It was 1949, and this was the last ship to leave Shanghai before the Communists seized full control of the city and sealed off avenues of escape. When I was growing up in Ohio, more than once I used to think, "But for the grace of God I would have been a Red Guard!" And, I would add in hindsight, "If not for the sheer determination, courage, and perseverance of our mom."

My dad was already in the U.S. on a one-year study and research grant at Ohio State University. He was prepared to return to China, but Mom wrote, "The Communists are taking over the country. Stay in America. I will find a way to get the children and myself out of China. We will join you in America."

I wonder now, given the chaos in Shanghai in those desperate final days, with everyone wanting to escape, how did my mom think she was going to get us out? Gold and contacts, for sure, but it required more than that. I know my mom as an inventive, smart, and determined person, and she found a way.

I have always been puzzled why my memories of that trip from Shanghai to Hong Kong are so dim. Then, it occurred to me. I had had a high fever and was very sick on the ship. There was no medication, and hardly anything to eat. I remember mom feeding me "xi fan," a thin rice porridge, the only thing I could swallow and the only food available.

Our small ship was dangerously overcrowded. After all, it was the last to escape from Shanghai. We were among the lucky ones; we had a bunk. One bunk for the four of us to share, so we could take turns sleeping, and we had a place to sit during the day. Luckily, it was also the top bunk and next to a porthole. Thank goodness for some fresh air! The other bunks were also packed with bodies and even more people were sleeping on the floor, making it almost impossible to walk. I shudder to think of those below deck, and their condition.

The trip from Shanghai to Hong Kong normally took about four days, but it took us seven days. A few days out to sea we ran into a terrible storm. Everyone had to throw their one small piece of baggage overboard to keep our ship afloat. The choppy seas made everyone sick. The stench in our overcrowded space was unbearable. Being Christians, we prayed. Miraculously we made it safely to Hong Kong.

In the Chinese tradition, family is paramount, and you always helped family members in need. Thus it was the four of us squeezed into the already cramped apartment of my Dad's younger sister with her husband and three children. My siblings and I were close enough in age to our three cousins to play together, though I think we fought as much as we played. Hong Kong's summers are unbearably hot and humid, and of course we had no air conditioning.

From the moment we arrived in Hong Kong, Mom was on a mission to secure visas for us to join my dad in America. I have memories of mom setting out early every morning to take the bus to the U.S. Consulate. The line at the Consulate stretched for blocks. She'd stand in the oppressive heat all day, to no avail. By the time they closed for the day, she still hadn't gotten in the door! This went on for days… and weeks. Finally one day she made it inside before the Consulate closed. With Dad already in the U.S., Mom was able to obtain visitor's visas for us. Three months after landing in Hong Kong, we set sail for America, Mom's dream.

This time our ship, the President Wilson, was like heaven! It was a wondrous contrast to the pathetic little ship that had enabled our escape just a few months earlier. We had an entire room to ourselves, with two bunk beds, so we each had our own bed! This, after sharing beds and being squeezed in my aunt's tiny apartment. The ship seemed enormous, and my older sister, younger brother, and I never tired of exploring. Going to America on the President Wilson was a fun adventure!

"The China Doctor"

He stood slightly stooped and had a serious but kind and wrinkled face, topped with a mound of grey hair. He was already in his late sixties at the time we escaped from Shanghai. I feel very certain that, if it were not for Dr. Harry Miller, our family would not have made it to America. It was he who sponsored my Dad for the one-year study and research grant to Ohio State University. And it was his contacts and connections that helped Mom to secure our passage and escape on the last boat leaving Shanghai.

A biography was written about Dr. Miller titled *The China Doctor*. Harry Miller first went to China as a Seventh-day Adventist missionary doctor at the age of twenty-four, in 1903. Over the next seventy years he served at various times in China, devoting over thirty years of his life to serving the Chinese people. His work benefited not only the Chinese, but tens of thousands all over Asia through the medical institutions he established, such as clinics, sanitariums, hospitals, and nursing schools.

Dad met Dr. Miller while attending the church-sponsored college, and Dr. Miller took a liking to Dad's earnest and extroverted personality and became a mentor and friend. Dad was a CPA and rose to become the Shanghai regional treasurer for the church's significant operations in Shanghai. Mom was a registered nurse and worked with

Dr. Miller in the Seventh-day Adventist hospital. One of his hallmarks was speed, and Mom was one of the few operating nurses who could keep up with him as he whipped through an operation. As a child, I remember Mom telling some interesting and comical stories about working with the colorful Dr. Miller. Once, he started to sew up the incision before Mom had a chance to remove all the surgical sponges!

Dr. Miller was not only a physician but also an inventor and entrepreneur. China was a very poor country in those days, with widespread starvation and malnutrition. He especially wanted to help babies and children, so he invented soy milk and other soy products. To my knowledge, these were the first soy products of their kind in China.

We children were the early "beneficiaries" of Dr. Miller's efforts. Mom would hold up a glass and declare, "You need to drink a glass of this every day to be healthy." I don't know if Mom truly believed this or just wanted to keep the peace with Dr. Miller. It looked and tasted like white goo! I had to hold my nose to gulp it down. Dr. Miller also created a soy burger and soy hot dogs. None of it tasted good in those early days. But that didn't deter Dr. Miller.

Our first home in America was, literally, the factory for Miller Foods. After our long drive across country in a van, we ended up in Mt. Vernon, Ohio, home of Miller Foods. When we arrived, there was no other place for our family of five, so we slept in this enormous 'room' right in the factory. It was dark and cold!

Kids are resilient and, for us, the factory was a great playground during the day—we ran around and played hide-and-seek among the stacks of boxes. My younger brother was four, and he had a great time riding around on his tricycle. Fortunately, a place was found for us to share a house with another family, just before the cold Ohio winter set in.

Dr. Miller was a larger-than-life figure, with a long list of accomplishments, but he remained a humble person and always gave all the glory and credit to God. Someone who knew him over the decades wrote an article about him and put it well: "He has served presidents and paupers, coolies and cabbies, senators and sots."

For our family, and I'm sure for countless others, Dr. Harry Miller was truly a godsend.

Attitude and Adapting

As I think back, our early years in America could not have been easy for Mom. After all, she had grown up in a privileged household, and even after her marriage to my father did not need to do any housework or cooking, as help in China was plentiful and cheap. Overnight, Mom faced tackling all the household chores in addition to learning skills such as perming hair for my older sister and me, sewing our dresses for school, canning fruits and vegetables for the winter, working part time as a nurse's aide during the day, and attending school at night to learn English.

Through the years, no matter what hardships and difficulties my parents faced, I never once heard them complain, unless it was Mom complaining about Dad. Mom was fortunate Dad had a lot of patience, she was the quick tempered one. In her twenties Mom had started to lose her hearing as a result of an infection and no antibiotic treatment, as this was during the war years with Japan. Dad used to say, "It's hard for your mom, she doesn't hear things, or only part of it." Dad was the extrovert, who loved being with people, while Mom was the introvert, preferring to keep to herself, partly due, no doubt, to her hearing loss.

The American dream for my parents was to be able to send all four of us (my sister Beth was born in Ohio) through college and to have the independence and freedom of owning their own business and home. Like so many immigrants, through years of hard work and perseverance, as well as a few failures, they were eventually able to achieve their American dream.

Throughout the years they owned several small businesses, including a Chinese restaurant in Akron, Ohio and several small motels after that. The last one, which they owned for thirty-three years, was in historic and picturesque Williamsburg, VA. Dad very ably took care of the business side as well as getting out and meeting people in the community, while Mom, with her eye for detail, made sure every room was spic-and-span and in top condition. But she also had good business acumen, which she displayed for the many years she ran the business with my brother after Dad passed away at the relatively young age of 76. As the property aged they were proud to maintain their AAA rating.

Both my parents taught by example. Neither ever told us, in so many words, to study hard, get good grades, and excel in school. They simply let us know, by example and in their own way, we were expected to do our best. For my part, I always felt a responsibility to my parents to excel, I wanted them to be proud of me. This feeling and attitude was an important motivator and touchstone for me growing up.

Equally important, as far back as I can remember, I felt a responsibility to be a good example of being Chinese American. Here we were, the only Asian American family in a small town in Ohio. How did I get this sense of responsibility, from such a young age? I don't know. It seems this was simply always a part of me, of my being. And it remains so to this day.

A True Patriot

I don't know when my mom first had the dream of coming to America. Maybe it was through stories she heard as a child, or while attending a church sponsored nursing school, which had some American staff. The Seventh-day Adventist church had quite a presence in Shanghai, with its college, nursing school, hospital and clinic.

Chinese words are made up of two characters, each with its own meaning, thus giving the word a depth often beyond the English translation. The two characters for the Chinese word "crisis," "wei ji," mean danger and opportunity. So often in a crisis we focus solely on the danger, and don't see the opportunity. Our family faced a crisis in the summer of 1949, and there was real danger. Mom, however, saw the opportunity in the crisis—an opportunity to escape, to come to America to re-unite with my Dad, and to start a new life in a country that offered freedom.

In the aftermath of the tragedy of September 11, 2001, Mom proudly flew a small American flag on her car. Every Fourth of July you'd see the American flag on her front lawn. She was an ardent Reagan supporter, as was I. Although we never specifically discussed this, it's my sense that Mom's love for America may have been even greater than her love for China. At the very least, she loved both equally. America suited her…she was fiercely independent and proud, and loved freedom.

I am certain that, if not for Mom's determination, courage, and ingenuity, we would not have escaped in 1949 and made our way to America. Her great love for this country, as well as her pride in being American, have been passed on to me and my siblings.

A Daughter's Dream

*Dreams come a size too big so
we can grow into them.*
- Josie Bisset

First Taste of America

I was standing on the deck of the President Wilson, under a sunny blue sky, somewhere in the middle of the Pacific. A young man, probably in his early 20s, caught me staring at what he held in his hand. He smiled and offered it to me. I guessed it was something to eat, but how, without a spoon or chopstick? He pantomimed and I thought I understood. I took a bite, made a mess on my face, but never mind. It was love at first taste—my first ever ice cream cone.

Growing up in Ohio as Seventh-day Adventists, we'd attend church on Saturdays. After church, our weekly family outing would often be a leisurely drive somewhere, and the special treat for my two siblings and me would be a stop along the way at our favorite Dairy Queen. As Marcel Proust made famous in "the episode of the madeleine,'" a taste can bring back a flood of memories.

I think back to that late summer of 1949, on the President Wilson. Somewhere in the Pacific Ocean between China and America, I had my first taste of America. It was sweet; it was delicious. And what a wonderful way for me to start my new life as a proud Chinese-American.

Magical First Christmas

As children in Shanghai, my sister and I use to perform at church, singing hymns such as "Jesus Loves Me." We celebrated Christ's birthday at church, but Christmas as a holiday was not celebrated in China until recent years.

I can still picture my very first Christmas in America. The house we shared with another family was only a short walk from the enormous home of Dr. Miller. His daughter Maude and grandson Stanford lived with him. Stanford was a few years older than my older sister, and naturally was the 'leader' in our various outdoor adventures.

Dr. Miller invited our family to spend our first Christmas at his home. As we entered his house, I was awestruck by the gigantic, majestic tree, beautifully decorated and twinkling with a thousand little lights. It felt like a magical tree. After dinner, we gathered around the tree and Dr. Miller handed each one of us a beautifully wrapped gift. None of us had ever seen such beautiful paper, and we couldn't bear to rip it. We tried very hard to remove the scotch tape without tearing the paper.

I very carefully unwrapped my box. Cradled in it was the first doll I had ever seen. She had a beautiful porcelain face and eyes that could close and open. I was in heaven! I have a photo of my oldest granddaughter a few years younger than I was then, hugging her doll at Christmas. It brings back memories of my magical first Christmas.

Little Green Schoolhouse

In my mind's eye, I can clearly see this little one-story schoolhouse with a dark green roof. It stood all by itself on the corner lot, the front facing the small road, the back leading to a modest playground with a few swings, see-saws, and a small merry-go-round. It was not a public school; it was a Seventh-day Adventist church school for grades one through eight, and this was where I attended school for my first eight years.

The classes were small, about ten to twelve students each, and each teacher taught two grades, which shared the same classroom. I always listened in to the upper class and by fifth grade I was doing all the sixth grade classwork. I remember my teacher, Miss Yingling, a rather hefty old maid, sitting in our living room telling my parents I should remain with my class and not skip a grade. I sure wish she hadn't done that.

Years later, when my son was born after my junior year at Barnard College, I thought, "If not for Miss Yingling, Jeff would have been born *after* I graduated, and I would have been spared my very challenging senior year as a full-time student, mom and housewife."

Even though I knew I was 'different' being Chinese among all those white faces, I never felt this was a disadvantage. I looked around at the other little girls in my class. Joyce and Patty were pretty with wavy brown hair, and Lois was a cute blonde, and they often wore new dresses to school. I knew I certainly couldn't be the prettiest girl, and I knew I couldn't be the best dressed girl, so I decided I'd be the smartest girl instead. This was something I felt I could achieve.

Even as a young child, I felt it was my responsibility to be a 'model student,' to positively represent Asians and Chinese in our small town where we were the only Asian family. Being only seven, I don't think this was a conscious thought, just something I simply felt deep within me. This feeling of both pride and responsibility being Chinese American was something of a double-edged sword. On one hand it motivated me to always do my best, to work harder; on the other hand I put tremendous pressure on myself and never gave myself any credit.

After years of saving and living frugally, we were finally able to move out of the house we shared with another family. Dad bought a house on a nice corner lot with a vegetable garden and huge yard. The day before a test I'd go into the dark basement, sit at a table my Dad had put there for me, bare except for a desk light, and I'd literally be there till bedtime, going upstairs only to eat. If I received anything less than 100, I'd be disappointed in myself.

I graduated eighth grade as the valedictorian, with straight As for all eight years—well, I did get one A-. As valedictorian it was my role to give a speech. As I was writing this story, I was wishing I had a copy of my speech. Then, unbelievably, I came across it a few days later. I felt as if I had found a treasure. I held in my hands two sheets of age-tinted notebook paper, filled with very neat handwriting, much neater than my current handwriting. I gave all the credit to our parents, and to God, but forgot to thank our teachers. That day, standing tall behind a podium delivering my first speech, my love for public speaking was born.

Growing Up American

"You mean you didn't speak Chinese at home?" Over the years I've often been asked this question and, somehow, it usually sounds a bit accusatory, as if my parents neglected their duty. And likely I sound a bit defensive when I reply, "This was many years ago. We grew up in a small town in Ohio, and we were the only Asians. My siblings and I just wanted to be American."

I'd go on to explain my mom spoke very little English, and by speaking English at home we helped her. Thinking back, I have no idea when she even found the time to study English outside the home, but she learned to read fluently and had beautiful handwriting, though her spoken English always carried an accent.

In 1958 Dad became partners with Mr. Wong in his Chinese restaurant, Wong's Garden, and we moved to Akron, Ohio. As Chinese New Year approached, the local paper in our town, the *Akron Beacon Journal,* contacted Dad and asked to do a story on our family celebration of this Chinese holiday, which was gradually gaining some public attention.

When the day arrived, a reporter came to the house to interview Mom and Dad, and a photographer took pictures of the family. I had long forgotten about this, until I recently came across the old, yellowed clipping with the photograph. At that time there were very few Asians in Akron. In fact, I don't remember any at Buchtel High School, which I attended. I like to think having this story in the local paper helped to spark some interest in the community in an important aspect of Chinese tradition and culture being kept alive by one Chinese American family.

As we grew up, left home, and dispersed, it became rare for us to get together at Chinese New Year's. It wasn't until I lived in Beijing, more than forty years later, that I fully realized and appreciated just how important, almost sacred, this holiday is for the Chinese. People will, literally, drop everything and do anything, including stand for several days(!) on a bus or train, to celebrate the Lunar New Year with their family. Had I more fully appreciated the importance and significance of this holiday to my mom, I would have made more of an effort to celebrate it with her over the years. But Mom, being the way she was, never wanted to 'interfere' with our lives, nor did she wish for us to feel guilty, so she downplayed the importance of the holiday to her.

A Touching Insight

Soon after we arrived in America we started school. It wasn't long before my sister and I begged Mom to cut off our pigtails and let us have curly hair like the other little girls at school. Having a perm in a beauty salon was totally out of the question. Bless her heart, my mom had never given a home perm in her life, but she tackled this in stride. For years my sister and I had home perms twice a year. It was a long, multi-step, arduous process and it was always sheer torture. Mom would wind the curlers good and tight, and my head felt like a porcupine! Sometimes the perm turned out OK, but other times it was 'overdone', and I would live with frizz until the perm loosened. The photo on my citizenship paper shows me with a new perm—a sight (not) to be seen.

Along with all the new skills Mom needed to learn for life in the U.S., she learned to sew. This too, was born of necessity. In the early years there was no money for store-bought school clothes, so she made the dresses for my sister and me. Of course, I also got all the hand-me-downs from my older sister. For someone who taught herself to sew, Mom did a decent job, but somehow the dresses always had a homemade look. Nonetheless, I always wore the dresses proudly, especially if it was a new one.

A few weeks after I'd written about my home perms and homemade dresses, a startling realization came to me. I've never questioned why it's always been important to me to look polished and "put together." I simply accepted that this is the way I am, and I've received many compliments along the way. Out of the blue, it struck me that inside the well-coifed and stylishly dressed woman, there's a little girl who remembers her frizzy hair and homemade dresses, and subconsciously determined that, one day, she'd have great hair and be well dressed!

Reflection: *This was a touching insight for me. I never knew why my hair and clothes have always been such a focus for me, why they are such an important part of my self-image. Having this* *realization and insight enables me to have more self compassion and self understanding, less self judgement, and to be more fully accepting of myself just the way I am.*

Prejudice

"Growing up in Ohio and during your career years, did you ever face prejudice, and if so, how did you handle that?" This question was posed by a psychiatrist attending my talk at the Mountain View Library in December, 2013: "Bridging Two Worlds—Proud To Be Chinese American." I thought for a moment, then replied, " I'm sure there were, while growing up and later in the corporate world, but I've always chosen to see the glass as half full, not half empty. I was likely aware of the prejudice, but I chose not to put my attention on it. In a sense, I did not even 'see' it. I certainly didn't let it affect me."

A few instances are buried deep, but come to mind as I reflect. In high school I was a majorette and part of the "in group." After the football games we'd go together to the various parties. One girl was on the fringe of our group. Her dad was an executive at one of the major tire companies (Akron used to be called the 'Tire Capital" of the world) and they lived in a house that could only be called a mansion. She threw several large parties during the year, and everyone in our group was invited—everyone except me. The first time this happened I made excuses in my mind; maybe she didn't have my telephone number or maybe it was an oversight. Then it happened a second time, and a third time. I could no longer kid myself. She was in my chemistry class; should I say something to her? I agonized privately over this and debated with myself for days. In the end, I let it pass. I knew in my heart why she had not invited me.

There was another incident during my high school days, but this was a very different situation. At a party, I met a popular, good-looking boy who attended another school. Soon after we met, and to my surprise, he asked me to a dance at his school, which I happily accepted. About a week before the dance, he called and asked if he could come by the house as he wanted to talk to me. When he arrived, he suggested we go for a walk. As we walked, he explained, in words and a tone that were so kind, he couldn't take me to the dance after all. I don't remember his exact words, I don't even remember his name, but I remember it was a very touching conversation. I could feel how ashamed and sad he felt at having to break our date, because his parents objected.

One other incident comes to mind. As a freshman at American University, I decided to participate in Rush Week, thinking I might wish to join a sorority. There was one where I really liked the sorority sisters and felt welcomed and accepted. I was overjoyed at getting the good news from this sorority. A week later, one of the sisters came to my dorm to break the news to me. "Dinah," she said, "the national sorority turned down your name." She didn't have to spell out the reason. It was clear to me they did not accept Asians, though this, of course, was not a written policy. From joy to hurt and disappointment. I decided to put it behind me—joining a sorority was not for me after all.

I'm sure there were incidents of subtle prejudice during my work years, which I chose to ignore. In some ways being a Chinese American woman in the corporate world in the 1980s was a 'double-edged' sword. At my first job after my MBA, my boss's boss remarked as he passed me in the hall, "They got two points for you." At first, I was puzzled. What could he mean by that? Later, it dawned on me he was referring to Human Resources—getting a point for hiring a minority, and another point because I was a woman. I never believed, not for a moment, that getting points had anything to do with me getting hired.

A Dream Come True

I was rummaging in a storage box one day, and unexpectedly came across an old weathered "scrapbook." It was a *Look* magazine dated September 23, 1952, I was ten years old then. As a child, I loved looking at the *Look* magazines. They were oversized, twelve inches by fifteen inches, and filled with photos and pictures, especially of movie stars and high society. We lived very frugally in the early years, and there was no money to buy a real scrapbook. I improvised, and pasted pictures from other old issues onto the pages of this one issue, which became my scrapbook.

Looking through it, I was struck by something. The theme seemed to be beauty, especially beautiful women and beauty queens, from Homecoming Queens to beauty pageant queens. There was a picture of the movie star Rita Hayworth. In junior high I gave myself the middle name Rita, because she was glamorous, and I wanted to have a middle name like all my friends.

I'm very sure I did not consciously aspire to be a "beauty queen"—that would have seemed way too impossible for a plain little Chinese girl with frizzy permed hair and homemade dresses. Yet I must have harbored a secret, subconscious desire to one day be pretty, and maybe even wear a crown.

The memories come back. I had transferred to Buchtel High School from Mt. Vernon Academy my sophomore year, after my parents moved to Akron. In my junior year I was President of Y-Teens, an all-girls service club, I wrote for the school paper, maintained top grades and was a majorette. Still, much to my surprise, someone nominated me to be one of four candidates for Homecoming Queen. This was the big event of the football season and of the year, and the entire school voted. I remember sitting in my homeroom when the announcement was made over the PA system. The whole room broke into enthusiastic applause.

In that moment, it felt unreal. This was a dream I didn't dare to dream, coming true!

Until this time, I never "connected the dots." Looking at my childhood scrapbook made from an old *Look* magazine, I now realize that, even as a child, I had dreamed "the impossible dream," which later came true. I must have spent many happy hours making my scrapbook and subconsciously dreaming that one day I'd wear a crown. Wow, this is an important lesson and insight for me, right here, right now, sixty-one years later.

This plain little Chinese girl with frizzy home perms and homemade dresses grew up to be the Homecoming Queen at Buchtel High School. And the summer before my senior year I was crowned Miss Akron, in a contest sponsored by the Junior Chamber of Commerce.

Recalling these forgotten memories, buried deep in my heart for over half a century, brings tears to my eyes—tears of joy for that little girl who wanted so much to be the All-American Girl and make my parents proud. This was such a motivator and touchstone for me growing up. My parents worked so hard for my siblings and me, to give us the opportunity to live the American Dream.

Reflection: *Looking back, with the perspective of many decades, I feel proud that, as a Chinese American girl in the fifties, in a Midwestern town, I helped to demonstrate that it was possible to break through any prejudicial barriers. My victory wasn't just for that plain little girl; my victory was also for all Asian Americans.*

Living Someone Else's Dream

To not dare is to lose oneself.
- Soren Kierkegaard

You Did It Backwards!

"You did it backwards!" someone exclaimed, after I briefly described my career path. I hadn't thought of it that way before, but she was right. I was attending the 20th Reunion of my graduation from my *alma mater*, the all-women Barnard College, Columbia University, in New York City. The room was packed for this popular breakout session focused on career and parenthood, the ever-present issues of timing for a woman and the effect this has on her career. Contrary to the other alums in the room, I hadn't started my career until I was thirty-six—because I started my family when I was twenty-one.

I never imagined I'd marry while still in college, but he emphatically stated that if I didn't marry him, he'd go back to Hong Kong and I'd never see him again. It worked! We'd met the spring of my freshman year, when I went to visit my sister at the University of Pennsylvania. At the time, I was in the School of International Studies at American University in Washington, D.C. and had planned on a career in the Foreign Service. He was finishing up his Masters from Wharton Business School. After we were engaged, I transferred from American University to Columbia University. We were married after my sophomore year, and our son was born after my junior year. To say I had a challenging senior year would be a gross understatement.

I started my fall term in September, and that's when my morning sickness started. It lasted for five months, and it was bad. It's hard to concentrate in class when you're feeling nauseous! At lunchtime I couldn't even walk into the school cafeteria without gagging.

We were living in Riverdale, north of Manhattan Island, and I'd drop my husband at the subway which he took to work near Wall Street. I would then drive down the Henry Hudson Parkway to Morningside Heights, where Barnard College and Columbia University were located. I'd be in classes till mid/late afternoon, after which I'd head back home, do chores, cook dinner, then pick him up from the subway. I must have done my homework mostly in the evenings. How did I have the energy? Pregnancy and not enough sleep made it very hard to stay awake in my morning classes, and I didn't want to be drinking coffee at that time.

My major was Economics, and a number of my classes were on the Columbia University campus, across Broadway from Barnard, in those large theater-like tiered classrooms. I couldn't help but feel self-conscious, walking into those classes of mostly guys, as my stomach got bigger and bigger. There wasn't another pregnant student in sight.

As difficult, physically, as it was for me to be carrying a full load of classes while pregnant, it was that much more difficult after the baby arrived. Jeff was born a week after my final exams. Thank goodness he waited for that! When I first looked at him, he had this worried look on his face, and I always thought my exams must have affected him. Happily, after a few days the worried look disappeared.

When I first learned I was pregnant, it never crossed my mind I wouldn't finish my last year at college. It was simply a matter of how could it be done? Fortunately, my parents were living in Bronxville, about twenty minutes from us. I arranged for all my classes to fall on Monday, Wednesday, and Friday, between 10 a.m. and 2 p.m. and while I was at school, my mom looked after Jeff. As soon as I got home, Mom left so she could be home when my younger sister (in junior high) got home. There was one class that met everyday, Mandarin, so that had to wait until summer. Sadly, lacking one course robbed me of being able to wear the cap and gown and walk down the aisle in June.

My husband had been raised in Hong Kong, and despite six years of college and grad school in the U.S., he'd grown up with a different norm, and there was no way he was going to help with any household chores. His job and responsibility were to support the family, and my job was everything else. Thus, I was a full-time student, mother of a newborn baby, and housewife with cooking, cleaning, washing and ironing—there was no budget for a sitter or help in those early years.

I have no idea how I managed it all! Once a week, either Saturday or Sunday, I'd have my "time off," to go to the library for a few hours to do research for my senior thesis. My adviser was the well-known economist, Raymond J. Saulnier, who was Chairman of the Council of Economic Advisers (CEA) from 1956-1961 and a professor at Barnard for thirty years. It was under his counsel and guidance that I wrote my senior thesis on the power and influence of labor unions and their effect on the economy. I was very proud I achieved honors in my major, Economics.

Reflection: *My senior year at Barnard really put me to the test at a young age. I've always believed, "Where there's a will, there's a way." Even now, with more than seven decades behind me, if anyone asked me my proudest accomplishment in life, I'd say graduating from Barnard with Honors in Economics and a fifteen-month-old baby! There was never a moment's doubt about "doing it all" at the age of twenty-one.*

Five Countries in Fifteen Years

When I got married at the age of twenty, I didn't know that my husband's dream was to get a position in Asia, where he'd been born and had lived until the age of seventeen, when he came to the U.S. for college and graduate school. I had no idea I'd end up living overseas for fifteen years.

Jeff was my parents' first grandchild and they adored him. Nearly every weekend we'd go visit them at the motel they owned and operated in New Jersey, sometimes staying overnight. Jeff, aged two, would follow my dad around the motel, asking him questions, and my dad would just crack up. How I wish I could have recorded some of the grandpa/grandson exchanges.

But when Jeff was two-and-a-half, we left our home in Riverdale and moved to Hong Kong, the first of five Asian cities we'd live in over the next fifteen years. It was exciting, and scary, as I said goodbye to family and friends.

A new chapter in my life was beginning.

Back in those days, the 60s, companies only granted 'home leave' every two years, so Jeff was five by the time Mom and Dad saw him again. By this time Deb was nearly one; she'd been born in Kuala Lumpur, the capital of Malaysia. Nearly every two years we'd come back to the States for four to six weeks to visit family. Our family favorite was to stop in Hawaii on our way to the mainland. We'd be at the beach, enjoying our family vacation, and, invariably, after a few days, something would come up which 'required' their Dad's presence in New York. Off he'd go and we'd be left to finish the vacation on our own. We got used to it.

Over the fifteen years in Asia we came full circle, in a sense. Hong Kong was our second city after Singapore, then Kuala Lumpur, Bangkok, Manila, and back to Hong Kong again.

Sometimes I'm asked which place I liked the most. It's hard to answer, as each was so different and had its own charms and challenges. Singapore is a well-run operation, very efficient, and an easy place to live. 'Perfection,' however, can be a bit boring. Kuala Lumpur is lush, green, and idyllic, the perfect place for me to be pregnant and give birth to our daughter. Bangkok is a cacophony of sounds and sights, with possibly the worst traffic jams in the world. The ubiquitous temples are architectural beauties and the Thai people and culture are charming. Hong Kong is an international metropolis, sophisticated and fast paced, but immensely dense, packed with skyscrapers and throngs.

If I had to pick just one place, I'd say I enjoyed Manila and the Philippines the most because of the people, who are friendly and warm. I had a few good friends who spoke fluent Spanish and sometimes they'd lapse into Spanish, then realize I was lost, and revert to English. Had we stayed longer I would have studied Spanish.

Without hesitation, I'd say the pros far outweigh any cons of our many years living in Asia. Our son and daughter grew up at ease and comfortable in different cultures. Their classmates and playmates were from many different countries and backgrounds. They traveled the world at a young age. They learned to adapt easily to new cultures, surroundings, new schools and new friends.

Adaptability is an important and advantageous life skill.

As for me, I learned, sometimes the hard way, how to manage a household with up to a staff of four: cook, maid, driver, gardener. At times, I'm sure they were managing me! This was all very new for me, and learning the skill was not a naturally easy task. Without the support system of family and old friends, life in a foreign country can be daunting and lonely for expat wives, especially in the beginning. The husband is fully immersed in his work and frequently gone for periods of time, traveling the region.

The wife also takes on the role of social secretary, as business entertaining was an important part of a husband's position. This was especially true in Asia in those days. It was not unusual to give or attend cocktail parties for fifty or more, or sit down dinners for eight or more on a weekly basis, if not more than once a week. The parties were always held at one's home, entailing much planning and preparation.

This was one of my key roles as the wife of an executive on the rise. I quite enjoyed this role, and felt I played it with grace and aplomb.

Importantly, those years living in Asia were the beginning of my appreciation for, and understanding of, Asian culture. Little did I know then my fifteen years living in five distinct cultures helped prepare me in many ways for what was to follow in my life, my years as an international business executive traveling frequently to Asia.

You're Just Too American!

Growing up first in Mt. Vernon, Ohio, where we were the only Asian family, then in Akron, Ohio, where we were one of a handful of Asians, I very naturally became totally American in my speech, mannerisms, and behavior. An incident happened while we were living in Bangkok between a good friend and myself that turned into my 'wake up' call.

Carol and Ed were good friends whose three young children often played with our son, Jeff, then aged five. In those days in the 1960s there were relatively few foreigners, and lots of business socializing in the evenings with the wives, usually cocktail or dinner parties at the home. We all lived in comfortable houses with live-in staff, so entertaining was enjoyable and part of the expat lifestyle.

Carol and I were working together on some event, specifics long forgotten. What I do remember, so clearly, is that our discussion was getting increasingly heated, in danger of turning into an argument. In exasperation, she finally exclaimed, "Dinah, you're just too American!"

I practically jumped backwards in shock! Here was my blond, blue-eyed, American friend, accusing me, a Chinese American, of being too American. When I calmed down, the truth of what she said really hit home with me. At the time of this incident, I had only been in Asia for two years, and was just beginning my journey to becoming more 'Asian' in my thinking and outlook. Her remark made me realize I needed to become more sensitive to the Asian way of thinking and behavior, and be more Asian in my approach.

We learn lessons in life from unlikely sources.

Longing To Do More

Moving is what happens when you're married to an upwardly mobile husband—it's either a promotion or a new job. As with our prior moves, there always seemed to be a business trip that took him away, usually ten days, long enough to avoid the movers on both ends, and time enough for most of the boxes to be unpacked. Here I was, with two small children, managing all the details of day-to-day life, while he focused on climbing the corporate ladder. In this respect, we were a good pair. Indeed, from the outside looking in, we were the ideal couple.

This time we were moving from Bangkok to Manila. We found a brand new house in an upscale neighborhood in Makati. It looked a bit like a miniature White House, with four stately tall columns in the front, and an all-white stucco exterior. The backyard had an oval pool, and a gazebo with blue tile roof where I did not sit, as I preferred to sunbathe.

This was our fourth move in four years, and I'd become quite an accomplished interior decorator. It became a hobby and something I put a lot of time and energy into doing well, and received many compliments. Our landlord was impressed with the way I had enhanced his house with my decorating skills, and said so. It seems he found a reason to stop by regularly, and I quite enjoyed our conversations.

We soon became friends with our next door neighbor, who had four children, two boys about the same age as our son. They owned a vacation house on Balesin Island, and the father piloted his own plane for their weekend trips. Happily, we were invited along several times. I remember a number of fun and relaxing weekends on beautiful and peaceful Balesin, walking the beach collecting shells.

I've always loved the beach, the smell of the sea, and the sound of the waves. There's something both soothing and therapeutic, yet at the same time invigorating, in the rhythmic sound of the surf. My favorite activity was to take a long walk first thing in the morning, usually not quite sunrise, then again at the end of the day, definitely at sunset. Watching the sun go down in a blaze of colors and glory always buoyed and inspired my spirit.

During one of our trips to Balesin, I was walking along the beach, feeling an emptiness, despite my very full days. I wondered, "What's wrong with me? I live an ideal life, am married to a successful husband, have two great kids, household help and a driver. What more could I want?" And, unstated, even to myself, "What more do I deserve?" Still, my heart knew I needed more. Many years ago—it seemed a lifetime ago—I had planned and dreamed of a career, of becoming a foreign diplomat. That was no longer to be. But, there had to be something more I could do, something besides being wife, mother, and social hostess for an upwardly mobile husband.

There was no one I could talk to but the waves. I made several failed attempts to talk with my husband. Once more, I pushed my yearning aside.

A Life Changing Revelation

While living in Manila, I became friends with a small group of women who came from privileged backgrounds and were bilingual in English and Spanish. It was through one of them that I was introduced to a new concept that proved to be life-changing for me.

I had grown up a Protestant, attending a Seventh-day Adventist church school for nine years. For many years after that I did not attend church regularly. After marriage, and once we moved overseas, we started searching for a church wherever we lived, both for the community and for the children. Somehow, no matter which church we attended, none resonated with me.

I didn't feel connected to God. And God was this entity outside of me, greater than me, comprised of the Holy Trinity: God the Father, God the Son, and God the Holy Spirit. Private sessions with the pastor or minister still did not answer my many questions or my longing for a closer relationship with God.

One day, my good friend Bonnie invited me to accompany her to hear a talk by a Filipino woman who had just returned from studies in the U.S. Bonnie was vague about what the talk would be about; I think she wasn't sure herself. When we arrived at the meeting place, I was surprised to discover close to two hundred people. There was an air of expectancy as we waited for the speaker.

Out she strode onto the stage, a striking woman, dressed all in white: white shirt, white pants, white shoes. Her name was Charly Barretto. She launched right into her talk and spoke without a break for ninety minutes, all the while constantly writing on the huge whiteboard, writing as fast as she spoke. I'm a consummate note taker, and I could barely keep up with her.

At the end of her talk, Charly offered a two-day seminar, at a very steep fee. I wanted to sign up, but was concerned my husband would object. All those years as a married woman I did not have my own budget or bank account and had to ask for anything outside of household expenses.

This was 1970 and my very first spiritual seminar, the birth of my "new" spiritual awareness, culminating in where I am today. Listening to Charly those two days and taking reams of notes marked a turning point for me. I was intellectually drawn to what she was saying, but at the same time I thought she was speaking sacrilege. She was de-bunking the Holy Trinity as I had been taught and grew up believing. She proclaimed, "The Spirit is not outside of you, somewhere in the universe; the Spirit lives within each of you!" Forty years ago, this was definitely new thought, especially in Asia.

Since then, I've attended dozens of seminars, workshops, and conferences and heard speakers such as Marianne Williamson, Deepak Chopra and Wayne Dyer.

In many ways, Charly ranks right up there with them. She had a powerful presence and compelling delivery. She was highly articulate, fluidly speaking beautiful sentences as if they had been carefully composed. She could speak for hours without any notes. And she never seemed to tire or lose her energy in spite of her rapid-fire delivery and non-stop writing on the whiteboard.

I had so many questions. I wrote her multi-page letters, in long hand. This was way before personal computers. To my amazement and surprise, she wrote multi-page replies, patiently answering my doubts and confusion. Charly's teaching was based on Science of the Mind, whose founder is Ernest Holmes. The principle that really hit home for me at the time is that we ourselves are responsible for our lives, and for everything that happens in our lives. This responsibility is also our liberty—they are two sides of the same coin. We can no longer blame others—parents, teachers, bosses, spouses, or our circumstances.

If we wish to be free, we must assume and accept responsibility for our actions and our life.

At the time, forty-plus years ago, this was a startling revelation to me. I struggled to be willing to undertake extensive soul searching. I had been thoroughly indoctrinated with my traditional Protestant beliefs and what Charly said, no, declared, sounded so foreign to me that it bordered on heresy. But, at a soul level, I was ready for this. I had been searching and praying for answers.

Once I was able to assimilate this 'new thought' and concept, then accept this as my new truth, I felt exhilarated with a new feeling of freedom. I was so excited about this new revelation I wrote lengthy letters to my family and a few close friends. When we moved from Manila back to Hong Kong, I had long discussions with a few close friends. I was bursting to share the good news but despite my best efforts, I don't think any of them really got it.

I couldn't wait to share this wonderful new revelation with my parents. That summer, on home leave, we were visiting them at their motel in Williamsburg, Virginia. It was a small motel with twenty-eight units, on two levels, called Colonel Waller Motel. Its most advantageous feature was that each unit had a compact living room with a small kitchenette, making it a "suite" though that sounds much too fancy a description. Out of financial necessity, my parents lived in one of the units for seven years, while they rebuilt their lost savings due to prior bad investments.

The four of us—Mom, Dad, my husband and I—were all standing in their small living room. I had just passionately shared with them my new found belief, that we each are fully responsible for the outcome of our lives, thus able to create a life of our choosing. I went on to say, in a tone that was more a declaration, "So I believe I can do, and become, whatever I choose, from this point forward in my life." They just looked at me… Silence. I could see and feel their disbelief and doubt in what I had just said. And worse, in me!

I burst into tears, then sobbed and sobbed. How could they not believe me? How could they not be thrilled for me?

When I finally stopped crying, a new resolve was born in me. I realized, I believed, I absolutely knew, to my core, I could create my life, my future, as I wished it to be.

For the first time since my marriage, I felt empowered.

A Dream Of My Own

Dream loftly dreams, and as you dream,
so shall you become.
- James Allen

There Has To Be More

As a young seventeen year old I had a dream, to major in International Relations, take the U.S. State Department exam, then enter the Foreign Service. I was a proud Chinese American and I had a dream of serving my adopted country. That dream was dashed by my early marriage and by prematurely starting a family. For the next sixteen years I was living my husband's dream, of climbing the corporate ladder.

I didn't have a dream of my own. I didn't dare to dream.

Over a period of thirteen years we had moved five times, and had come full circle. After living in Singapore, Malaysia, Thailand and the Philippines, we were now living in Hong Kong for the second time. Over the years I had become a polished hostess, I was a natural at my role, and we entertained frequently. A couple's social life, especially in those days, played an important role in the husband's position and in the business community. In this respect we were good partners, as I actively aided his climb up the corporate ladder.

Why had we moved so frequently? Some of it was due to my husband's promotions, others to his change of companies. I became adept at relocating: packing, unpacking, getting the kids settled into new schools, hiring and training new household staff, and quickly becoming an active part of the expatriate community.

At some point while living in Manila, I started to feel I could not forever play the role of social hostess. I needed and wanted to do more, be more. Discussions with my husband were not encouraging or fruitful. He could not relate. "Dinah, you already have everything a woman could want. You're living an ideal life! Why on earth do you want a job?" This was in the 70s, when wives of successful men in Asia did not work. Their full-time job was to manage the household staff, the kids' schedule, and, very importantly, the social schedule.

What had happened to my dream of having a career before I got married? I was now in my mid-thirties; was it too late? Having never held a full-time job, what could I do? Where could I start? So many questions swam around in my head, and there was no one I could talk to. None of the wives of our friends worked; they wouldn't have been able to relate. My husband didn't want to discuss it; he thought I already had the ideal life.

When we moved back to Hong Kong from Manila, I initially set aside any thoughts of starting a career. I became active in several organizations, was the President of the Association of American University Graduates, played tennis, attended luncheons and kept busy. But, my heart knew, something was definitely missing.

The feeling of wanting—no, needing—to finally start my career kept growing stronger. A day came I could no longer ignore this deep yearning. I still had no idea where or how to start. At last, I decided to give banking a try. I had majored in Economics, in fact, graduated with honors, despite being a full-time wife and mom my senior year.

Why Do You Want A Job?

I was being interviewed by a middle-aged mid-level bank manager. Near the end of our interview, he asked the question that was burning on his mind. "Dinah, you're living the ideal life. You certainly don't *need* to work. Why do you want a job?" He was totally perplexed and highly skeptical.

I replied, "You don't understand. For me, this isn't just a job. This is the start of my career!" I pointed out I had majored in Economics from a top school, I was at ease interacting with business people, and I was ready to work harder than the next person. But all this aside, I believe it was my passion and conviction which helped me get this low-paying entry-level position.

Hooray! I got the job!

Wow, what a triumphant feeling, my first full-time job! I was finally embarking on my career.

My husband's reaction was muted. I think he thought he'd humor me, I'd get tired of it and it wouldn't last. One of my best friends at the time, whom we saw every weekend in our social circle, asked, without fail, "Dinah, are you still working?" with a tone expecting me to say that I'd gotten bored and quit. After about two months she finally stopped asking. Our friendship was never the same once I started working. The same was true with other of my girlfriends.

My starting position was at Chase Manhattan Asia Ltd., Chase's investment bank, a smaller operation than the retail bank. My first day on the job, I met my direct boss, a twenty-something Chinese American who'd recently graduated from Harvard Business School. I was his first employee, and not exactly what he expected. I don't remember if I actually said to him, "I won't hold your age against you if you don't hold mine against me," or, if this is something that simply went through my head. You can say we had our challenges, and I began the important lessons in 'how to manage your boss.'

Soon after I joined, I learned the career path at the bank required completion of a rigorous and demanding six-month full-time training program. Normally you spent at least a year at the bank, before being nominated, then selected, for this highly competitive program. One year! I didn't have time to wait a whole twelve months. I began a campaign on my own behalf to take the training program sooner.

After six months of proving myself at my job, the powers that be finally relented, but on the condition I continue to do my job. Participants in this elite program came from all over the Asia region, from Singapore, Korea, Taiwan, and Japan. This was a full-time program, and they were not expected to do anything else. I, on the other hand, was required to go back to the office for a full afternoon of work, after a full morning of classes. I did my three-four hours of homework in the evenings, after dinner with the family, and tried to work ahead on weekends. Of course I also worked a 'half day' on Saturdays, which, thanks to my boss, usually meant 2:00-3:00 p.m.

My Saturday work schedule interfered with our all-important social schedule, as during racing season we'd get invitations for the races at the Jockey Club, complete with catered lunch in the private box. Otherwise, I made sure my work did not interfere with other invitations while also carrying out our own previous entertaining schedule.

It wouldn't be the only time in my career when I held two jobs simultaneously. When you're in a hurry, catching up for having started fifteen years late, double duty helps!

Shoe On The Other Foot

After successfully completing the full-time six-month training program with excellent marks, I was offered a new position from a Vice President for whom I had done some work before he was promoted and transferred to the retail bank. What a pleasant change from my old boss. In my new position, I had my own portfolio of clients. Our group handled Chases's priority multinational accounts, and among my clients were names such as Mobil, Tetrapak, and Revlon.

I was feeling a bit nervous about my new position, as some of the top people in these companies were social friends, people we saw at cocktail parties and dinners. How would they react to me being their account manager? They'd mostly known me as Mrs. so-and-so. A few knew I'd been working at the bank, but most didn't. Nonetheless, one of the first things I needed to do was to phone each account to introduce myself and set up a courtesy meeting. Despite my apprehension, this initial phase of my job went smoothly.

Entertaining clients was part of my job. Chase had a very nice conference room, which also served as a private dining room. Rather than taking my clients out to a noisy restaurant, I preferred entertaining them this way, and it felt special to them. I would order a nice floral centerpiece, select the menu, and the staff would set the table with crystal, china, and silver. It did look impressive and the food was excellent as well.

One day, after I'd been in my position for a number of months, my boss said, "Dinah, I think it'd be nice for you to start inviting some of your clients out for dinner." What can you say when your boss makes a suggestion like that? Entertaining the client for lunch included only people from the company. But entertaining for dinner meant inviting the wife as well. This meant my husband would also need to come along—a whole new ball game for him.

When I mentioned this to my husband, he was not at all pleased. The whole idea seemed preposterous to him. What, he was to be the accompanying spouse at a business dinner for which I would be the host? It took some time and a lot of cajoling before I could finally arrange my first client dinner.

The dinner did not go very well. My client and I awkwardly kept the conversation going, but there was palpable tension in the air. It was clear my husband was uncomfortable and did not want to be there. It was the first, and last, time I entertained a client for dinner. I not only felt upset, I felt very hurt. I had been the supportive spouse all those years, entertaining and playing the role of hostess, importantly aiding his career. Now, I was starting my career, which was going well, and he was unwilling to be supportive.

My fledging career was putting an added strain on an already strained marriage and relationship.

A Kris Through My Heart

I opened the front door of my three-story split level home in Hong Kong as I had hundreds of times, but this time, my heart ached, and I felt like crying. I knew soon I'd be entering this beautiful home for the last time. Of the five homes we'd lived in over fifteen years, this was the first time we'd bought. Renovating and decorating this home was a labor of love. This time, instead of walking past my foyer and up the stairs, I just wanted to savor the moment, knowing it would soon end.

I wasn't only saying goodbye to a beautiful home that I loved, I was saying goodbye to a dream, to a marriage that I had once thought would last a lifetime.

I don't know when my husband and I began to grow apart, during his years of extensive business traveling, focused solely on climbing the corporate ladder. It happened slowly over the years, so I hardly noticed in the beginning.

Our son was seventeen and in the States for prep school. Our daughter, thirteen, was in junior high at the Hong Kong International School. The year before our divorce we often sat calmly and quietly late at night in our darkened living room, discussing our marriage and how we might put our relationship back on track. Though there was a part of both of us which still wanted the marriage to work, another part could see we'd grown apart over the years and our values were now different.

In preparation for our pending divorce, I decided I needed to go back to school to get my MBA. I had full intentions of being able to support myself rather than relying on an alimony. So now, on top of my job and the bank training, I also needed to study for my GMAT. I bought a book and proceeded to go through it on my own. I don't know why I didn't investigate classes. At any rate I had no time except late at night and on weekends. Despite feeling inadequately prepared, I somehow miraculously made decent scores on the GMAT, and was accepted to Columbia Business School. Columbia University was my alma mater, as I had received my B.A. from Barnard.

Looking back, I don't know how I managed to live through this period of my life without having anyone I could talk to about it. There was no one I felt I could confide in, to be a safe container, to just listen. And, it was just too painful to talk about. I felt so scared, so alone. I had to "put on a happy face" for work, for friends, and for the children. All the while I felt my insides falling apart, my long ago dream of "happily ever after" shattered!

At the same time, I knew, deep in my being, I had to go through this to save myself.

When we lived in Bangkok I saw, for the first time, a kris. It's a dagger or sword with jagged edges on each side of the blade. Going through my divorce was a kris through my heart.

A few years after my divorce, during a spiritual retreat, we were told to draw our life timeline, with peaks and valleys representing events in our life. When it came to my divorce, my pen dropped to the bottom edge of the paper, and would have continued down…down…

I stood at the edge of the precipice. It took every ounce of my strength, every ounce of courage and faith. Then I jumped, and the universe put ground beneath my feet.

Reflection: *The decision to seek an amicable divorce came straight from my heart and soul. My head would have had me stay in the seemingly ideal marriage, but the relationship left me empty on a deeper level. We diverged in our values, and in what was important to us. My spirit felt held back and held down, not able to soar. I made the hardest decision I've had to make in many life times…to free my soul.*

What Are You Going To Do?

"What are you going to do when you grow up?" asked the late Boris Yavitz, Dean of the Graduate School of Business at Columbia University as he opened his Welcoming Remarks to our Orientation Session. We were the incoming Class of Fall 1981, having chosen to take the accelerated program which would enable us to get our MBA in eighteen, instead of twenty-one, months by going straight through two summers without a break.

My mom thought I was taking on far too much. After all, I'd been out of school for sixteen years and was going through a divorce after eighteen years of marriage; I was moving halfway around the world, and I wanted to take a full load of classes and not even take a break. I did not want alimony. Instead, I received a one-time monetary settlement. I was now totally on my own, and time is money. Besides, I was in a hurry, making up for a late start.

Was it hard? You bet! Well, some of the classes were easy for me, like Marketing 101. I received an Excellent, and decided then and there not to major in Marketing. Why should I pay so much money to learn something so intuitive to me? Instead, I majored in Finance/Business Economics, definitely more challenging.

Reflection: *I don't know where this belief came from, but I definitely had an inclination to downplay and devalue what came easily and naturally to me, and instead, to value what was hard and took a lot of work. I wish I'd known then what I know now.*

Go with your strength!

Studies have shown you get far better results by putting your energy on enhancing your strengths than by trying to improve your weak points. So many of us get this backwards!

There were a few students who actually majored in "Entrepreneurship." I remember thinking, "What a waste of time and money! What can you do with a major like that?" Little did I know. Back then, the goal for most of us was the Fortune 500, investment banking or consulting.

Rip Van Winkle

Overnight, I went from a beautifully furnished and decorated 3,600 square foot split-level condo with floor-to-ceiling windows, spacious enough to entertain sixteen for a sit-down dinner, which we did twice every Christmas, to a small apartment shared with two other graduate students.

This was the summer of 1980, as I began my new life.

The day I moved in, I discovered I couldn't use either the kitchen or the bathroom without first thoroughly scrubbing both. My first task was to defrost the refrigerator, which had this enormous crust of solid ice. This required manual defrosting, with hot water and a knife, which acted as an icepick as I stabbed at the solid block. This took a few hours and resulted in frozen fingers. Then, on to the bathroom, which was nothing short of disgusting.

After I finished several hours' work in the kitchen and bathroom, I asked my new roommates, "What do you do for dinner?" They both stared at me blankly, as if I'd just come from Mars. I later realized this was a total non-issue, as they ate whenever and whatever.

One morning, I stepped out of my bedroom and saw a man coming out of our bathroom. I got the shock of my life! My roommate never even thought to mention her boyfriend was spending the night. I had no clue how quickly and how far the social mores had moved over the past fifteen years while I lived in Asia. This was culture shock and I felt like Rip Van Winkle waking up from a deep sleep. I told myself, "Welcome to the brave new world of life back in the U.S.!" And, New York City, at that.

Reflection: *Going from my married, very social life in Hong Kong straight into an intense, academically rigorous and challenging*

MBA program was therapeutic for me. I had no time to dwell on the life I just left behind, and I certainly had no free time on my hands. I had structure, objectives and goals, social interactions and eighteen months to acclimatize to life back in the U.S.

My Overlooked Diamond

After successfully getting my MBA from Columbia Business School, I was faced with the reality of getting a job. I still vividly remember a conversation I had at the time with my son and daughter. The three of us were having a reunion dinner in New York City. "Mom, we think you'd make a great TV anchor, like Connie Chung!" they enthused.

Some of you may remember her; she was a popular TV anchor in the early 80s. Coincidentally, we had the same hairstyle and even looked a bit alike. Upon hearing this from my children I retorted, "An anchor person, to broadcast the news, and interview people? I'm going to be the one being interviewed!" I practically felt insulted. After all, I was graduating from a top business school and my aim was to become an important executive of a Fortune 500 company.

They even told me that their Dad, my ex, had expressed a similar view. So here were the three people who knew me best in many ways telling me the same thing. They saw in me the attributes that could make for a good, maybe even great, TV anchor. And I, with my inflated ego, dismissed the 'preposterous' idea without another thought.

Why would being an anchor/broadcaster have suited me so well? I've been told I have the natural 'gift of gab'—an ability to talk to anyone, about anything. From the time I was little I loved to ask questions. I have a natural curiosity about everything, and a great interest in a variety of topics. In fact, I love variety, change, and the new. New ideas, new concepts, new inventions—anything new sparked my interest. Some years later I belatedly realized that speaking and communicating on different topics, with interesting people everyday, would have been an ideal fit for me. I would have loved it, and thus excelled.

Unfortunately, at the time, my ego blinded me to my own diamond.

The good news is that I did have a great opportunity to utilize some of my public communication skills during the three-and-a-half years I served as a senior official in President George H.W. Bush's administration, from 1989 to 1992. As one of the top senior appointed Asian Americans, I was often invited to speak to different government groups, especially during May, Asian Pacific American Heritage month. These keynote addresses would be delivered in front of several hundred people.

The other day when I came across some typed notes I saw, much to my surprise, I had given over two dozen speeches, most of them keynotes, and participated in numerous sessions and workshops as panel moderator or panelist. Some of my keynotes were: "Salute to Asian Business," "Women and Leadership: The Challenge and Opportunity," "Education, Dignity, Distinction and Advancement," "Unity in Diversity," and "The Best of Two Worlds: A Chinese American Immigrant's View." Sadly, I only have the complete typed notes of a few of the speeches.

One speech that stands out in my mind, because I have the news clipping, is a speech I delivered for the Swearing In Ceremony for new citizens in the Colonial Capitol at Williamsburg, Virginia on December 4, 1989. I spoke on what my U.S. citizenship meant to me. I shared the story of our family, like legions of other immigrant stories, of how the hard work and determination of my parents enabled us to achieve the American Dream. As I read my speech, I am inspired by my own words. Let me share a few lines:

"Whatever your desire is, you can achieve your goal, because you live in a country of freedom, you live in a country of choice, you live in a country of abundant opportunities. Look for opportunities—not for obstacles. Turn each stumbling block into a stepping stone to take you one step closer to your goal."

Now, a quarter of a century later, I find my words above to be less true. We have fewer freedoms, fewer choices, and fewer opportunities than we did twenty-five years ago. A sad, and alarming, trend.

It is with a tinge of regret and sadness that I overlooked my diamond. Put your ego aside, and be open to listening, both to external sources, as well as to deep within yourself. Listen to what those closest to you say, listen to associates and colleagues, and even listen to strangers. Others often see talents in us that we're not consciously aware of ourselves. By definition, our natural talents are so natural to us we usually don't give them a second thought, taking them totally for granted. We may even think everyone has similar talents, not realizing this is far from the case.

It's vitally important for us to share our diamond. Without sharing our diamond, we cannot feel totally fulfilled. There will always be a feeling of emptiness, a feeling of something missing. We are created this way, with a deep need, a soul imperative, to share our diamonds, our talents, in the service of others. The wonder and beauty of this is that our diamond is unique to us. Like our fingerprint, it's our soulprint.

It makes no difference if a hundred people sing the same song; they each will sing it their way, with their voice, their interpretation, their heart and soul. And those of us listening enjoy and appreciate the uniqueness of each singer.

Desire to discover your diamonds, then wear them proudly, show them off! Let them sparkle and shine, bringing light and joy to others as well as to yourself.

They Got Two Points For You!

"They got two points for you," he said, as we passed each other in the hall. He was my boss's boss, the Director of Investor Relations at Union Carbide. I was puzzled by this remark, what did he mean? It was not until some time later that it dawned on me. He meant the Human Resources department had gotten two points for me, one for being a woman, one for being a minority. Oh… Welcome to the corporate world. I found this remark more amusing than insulting and chose not to dwell on it. I never felt getting the points had anything to do with me getting hired.

This was my first post-MBA job, my first job in the U.S. and what I considered to be the beginning of my climb up the corporate ladder.

Throughout my corporate career, I spent next to no time thinking about being a minority woman in the workplace. As far as I was concerned, I was hired to carry out a job and I was prepared to give it 200% of my time and energy. Let me back up and tell you how I ended up at Union Carbide.

One reason I chose Columbia's Business School is because they offered an eighteen-month program, allowing you to go straight through two summers. I started in May 1980 and finished in October 1981. In the spring of 1981 companies began coming to the campus to interview. Unlike many of the students, I deliberately decided not to interview for investment banking or consulting. To me, these two industries did not need more MBAs. What industry did need MBAs? The old-line, traditional manufacturing industries. Need I say I was very idealistic (and somewhat unrealistic) in my younger days.

Besides not dwelling on being a minority woman, I chose not to dwell on the considerable age difference between me and my classmates, and later my colleagues. My classmates knew I was older, but they had no idea it was fifteen years or so. I made friends easily, was encouraged to run for elected office, and was elected to be the President of the MBA organization, "Distinguished Leaders Lecture Series."

One invited speaker was Alec Flamm, an Executive Vice President at Union Carbide. Flamm was the head of UC's industrial gases business and also responsible for Strategic Planning. I was very interested in Strategic Planning, and, had this been offered as a major, I would have chosen it over Finance. He spoke to us on the important role of Strategic Planning at Union Carbide. I was inspired by his talk, and decided to seek an interview.

The day after he spoke, I called his office and spoke with his assistant who relayed my message. I got an appointment for a meeting! An important lesson I learned the hard way in my first job at Chase Bank in Hong Kong was how to relate to and communicate with the "gatekeepers." This lesson served me well the rest of my career.

At the time, Union Carbide's corporate office was on Park Avenue, only a few blocks from Grand Central Station, a great location. The company was scheduled to move to its new headquarters in Danbury, CT. It was not until later I learned that, at the time I went for my initial meeting/interview, there was a hiring freeze in place. An exception had been made for me.

I arrived for my interview expecting to meet with the Strategic Planning people, but met instead with people from Investor Relations. I felt disappointed. "I had hoped to talk about a position in Strategic Planning," I said, in my characteristic forthright way. Bob, the Director, explained, "Strategic Planning deals with highly confidential information about the company and only hires people who've been with the company for many years." I hadn't thought about it that way, but I could see their point.

Surprisingly, for a Fortune 500 company, Union Carbide had a very small Investor Relations department: a Director, a Manager, and two secretaries. I was hired as Associate Manager (I had been adamant about having 'manager' in my title), reporting to Nick, the manager. Nick was a soft-spoken and mild-mannered person, very protective of his job and turf. Bob, the Director, was formerly the head of an operating unit, and now serving out his years until retirement.

Being the "low man on the totem pole," the new hire, as I had been at Chase, I was assigned all the "numbers crunching."

And, in Investor Relations, there were plenty of numbers to crunch! To this day I love my HP calculator. Union Carbide was a complex industrial manufacturing company, with five very different businesses/divisions: graphite electrodes, polyethylene, agricultural products, industrial gases, and batteries. I decided I needed to learn as much about the company as quickly as possible.

After reading all I could get my hands on, and about six weeks into the job, I called up the directors (below the executive vice presidents, senior vice presidents, and vice presidents) in the various businesses to introduce myself and requested twenty-thirty minutes of their time to ask some questions. As busy as they were, I didn't have anyone refuse, and often they ended up giving me forty-five to sixty minutes. Within two weeks I had spoken to more than a dozen operating managers and taken copious notes. I typed up the key points of my notes for my manager and director.

When I told Nick what I was doing, he said, "You can't do that! They're busy people, they've got better things to do than talk to you." For Nick, such action was unthinkable.

He'd been in the job for over five years, and had never spoken to most of the people I met with. As a result, after I'd been in Investor Relations for six months I knew more about the company than Nick, who'd been there nearly six years. As you can imagine, this did not go over well with Nick. Worse, he actively tried to undermine me. The details escape me now, purposely buried, I'm sure. It was not the first, or the last, time in my career a direct boss felt threatened by me.

Bob, the Director, once said to me, "Dinah, go in to Nick's office and ask him something, even if you already know the answer." I tried it, but the relationship with Nick remained strained.

After my round of company interviews and my memo, Bob asked me to make a forty-five minute presentation to a group of analysts (sell side) and institutional investors (buy side). By this time I had spoken to some of them over the phone, in my day-to-day interactions with Wall Street. But the idea of a formal presentation to a roomful of professionals who had followed Union Carbide for years and knew the company inside and out was a bit daunting, to say the least.

The day before my presentation I came down with a bad cold, but short of having a fever, I was determined to go ahead. This was a very unusual occurrence, and a first for Investor Relations. The regularly-scheduled presentations were always made by senior management, usually an operating head. Here I was, a new hire, an Associate Manager, making the presentation, and I was able to provide them fresh information and fresh perspectives, across the businesses. My presentation was well received. What a relief!

From day one, I never forgot my objective was to be in Strategic Planning, not Investor Relations. A few months on the job I asked how I could transfer ("forgetting" I had been told it took years). After my successful public presentation, the V.P. of Strategic Planning took notice, and I was allowed to split my time between the two departments. It often felt like I had two full time jobs! Often I was the first one in and the last one out.

It was my belief I had to be willing to do double duty if I wanted to get ahead quickly.

I remember once working out at 11 p.m. in the small workout room at the condo where I lived. Did I think my schedule was insane? Yes. But I thought this was the price I had to pay to catch up for my late start in climbing the corporate ladder. And I was fully willing to pay the price.

Reflection: *Writing this decades later, I feel there must have been a way I could have worked smarter, and not simply harder. Probably 120% would haves sufficed; it didn't need to be 200%. Was it appreciated? Maybe some of it, but certainly not all. A few times it occurred to me that I was simply setting high expectations for my performance, which I then needed to continually meet.*

Presenting to the Executive Committee

After six months of holding two jobs, I guess I passed the "test" and was offered a full-time position in Strategic Planning. Hooray! And I no longer had to report to Nick.

When I started to write about my experiences at Union Carbide, I was surprised how much I had accomplished in my two-and-a-half years. In addition to my day-to-day responsibilities I had been given a number of special projects, which I welcomed. These allowed me to display my abilities and talents. I loved tackling problems or projects that were new to me, giving me the opportunity to be creative.

Shortly after I joined Strategic Planning, my boss, the V.P., assigned me a project to identify why Union Carbide could never achieve its stated financial targets so important to Wall Street— ratios such as P/E (Price/Earning), ROI (Return on Investment), ROA (Return on Assets), and ROE (Return on Equity). For years the company had stated its financial ratio targets in its Annual Report and other company communications, and never even came close. I think this was finally getting embarrassing for the top executives, and the company needed to rethink their elusive financial targets.

Frankly, I had no idea where to start with this project! And I'm sure, neither did the V.P. I decided to look at a cross section of industries, from manufacturing to consumer goods. I then studied the companies in each industry, from the best performing to the worst performing. Getting information in those pre-Internet/Google days was not easy. I called up analysts who covered these companies to learn more about the industry and the companies. Amazing these busy and overworked analysts even took my call and sometimes gave generously of their time and knowledge. I collected and complied a mountain of data to analyze to see if I could establish any patterns or trends.

I ranked the industries, those that consistently performed well or better over time vs. those that were slow growth, whatever the economic cycle. The great insight was that there are companies that performed extremely well even in the slow-growth industries, and they showed similar characteristics to those companies that performed well in the fast-growth industries. This meant that being in a slow-growth industrial sector was no excuse for under performing.

This was my first solo project as a new member of the Strategic Planning department and I was a bit nervous as I made the presentation to my colleagues. There were five of us in the department, reporting directly to the V.P. The group's response was positive and they asked helpful questions. When the presentation was over, the V.P. said to me, "Dinah, I'd like you to present this to the Executive Committee." I was floored! This was the top circle of six men who ran this multi-billion dollar company.

On the day of the presentation, I was in the room with the Chairman & CEO, the five Executive Vice Presidents who headed the five major businesses, and my boss, the V.P. of Strategic Planning. I spoke for forty-five minutes, using flip charts and slides. There were some questions, and one

EVP who challenged one of my numbers. I stood my ground (later I sent him a memo with further proof of my fact).

As I watched the faces of these six men, they were not very expressive but they seemed impressed and surprised. At the time, I didn't think too much of what was happening. But here I was, a new hire, at manager level, making a forty-five minute presentation to the Executive Committee! Now that I think back, I did break new ground, not only for women, but for minorities. This was thirty plus years ago, Union Carbide was a very conservative "old school" industrial and manufacturing company. And having a woman MBA from an Ivy League school was a first, not to speak of a Chinese American.

Later I learned I had been referred to by some in the company as "the Dragon Lady." Characteristically for me, I chose to take this as a compliment.

Heart Over Head

When you're new in a company and haven't yet had time to forge strong relationships and have support, it can be very difficult to make a decision that goes against your superiors. In the spring of 1982, when I had been with the company only six months and was essentially holding down two jobs,

I was put in charge of an important project in preparation for the company's Annual Meeting. A high profile part of the Annual Meeting is when the CEO takes questions from the Shareholders in attendance. One never knows what kind of questions will come up, and sometimes they can be both detailed and tricky.

To prepare for this, all the various businesses of the company were required to submit answers to possible questions that might be asked. I was put in charge of gathering the lengthy answers, following up on replies, then editing and organizing all the replies. Often the answers were so long-winded there was no way to get it on a 5x7 card and no way the CEO would be able to glance at it for facts and figures. I edited all the cards, to make them clear and concise. Many phone calls were required to chase down tardy responses and to clarify confusing and obtuse answers.

On the day of the Annual Meeting, as the questions were being asked, I (and one other person) would pick out the card with the best answer and the card would then be transmitted electronically and show up on a monitor on the podium, so the CEO would have the facts and figures he needed. This was the advanced technology at the time.

There was a problem. I had a reunion trip planned with my fourteen-year-old daughter, then living in Hong Kong with her Dad, the week before the Annual Meeting. When I told my boss, and his boss, they matter-of-factly said, "Dinah, you need to cancel your trip and re-schedule for after the

Annual Meeting." I was floored! How could I do this to my daughter and myself?

We were planning to meet in Hawaii, halfway between Hong Kong and the east coast, where I was. Re-scheduling our reunion would be difficult, given my daughter's school schedule. The thought of canceling a trip to see my daughter whom I hadn't seen for a year made me feel so sad. I was in a real dilemma. I had only been at U.C. for six months, and this was my second major project. My head told me to postpone my reunion with my daughter, to listen to what the bosses wanted.

I searched my heart, and my heart said, "Go on the trip; you need to see your daughter." I told my bosses, "I'm not canceling my trip. I'll get everything done before I leave, and be back in time to oversee this for the Annual Meeting." They were not happy! But I had spoken with conviction and certainty. And, by now, they knew I performed and kept my word.

Sure enough, the Question & Answer part of the Annual Meeting went smoothly, as I had practically memorized the dozens of cards which I had edited and organized into topics. Whenever I've thought back to this challenging situation early in my career, I've been so glad I listened to my heart. Unfortunately, I have not always listened to my heart.

Reflection: *I've learned the hard way that when my head and heart don't agree, I should always listen to my heart. The heart* *has a wisdom and knowing way beyond the head. This is a lesson I'm still learning...*

Resigning On Principle

I'd just received my second annual performance evaluation and I was both delighted and dismayed. Delighted I'd received such high ratings: Outstanding and Excellent in all categories of performance. Dismayed, because the pay raise was still only a paltry three percent! This had happened to me the year before, when I was in Investor Relations. I don't know why I thought it could/would be different this time, but I fully expected a much higher raise. This time, it finally hit me that in a large, very conservative company, strictly managed by the book, it would likely never change. Further, this led me to see that my entrepreneurial self did not really fit into this kind of corporate environment and corporate culture.

When I joined U.C. I had envisioned being there for many years, maybe my whole career, having the opportunity to hold different positions and climbing the corporate ladder. I'd been there two plus years, had held two positions, with one promotion—not bad. Still, I saw the handwriting on the wall for much slower progress than what I had envisioned or desired.

After much soul-searching, I wrote a letter of resignation, addressed to the EVP who had referred me, the Director of Investor Relations, and my current boss, the VP of Strategic Planning.

By now everyone who knew me and had worked with me knew me to be fearless and unconventional. I imagine when the three executives received my resignation letter they were surprised, yet maybe not completely. When does a newly minted MBA at the manager level write a resignation letter to the EVP at a multi-billion dollar company? I felt I owed him an explanation for my resignation, since he had made it possible for my initial interview and had given me important tacit support during some rough going with Nick in Investor Relations. I wanted him to hear my reasons in my own words, not filtered through a second-hand source.

The amazing thing is that my boss, the V.P. of Strategic Planning, threw a farewell party for me, despite my strongly worded resignation letter. He organized a farewell dinner at his country club, including all the wives. Thinking back, this was likely on his own tab, given that it was his own country club, and the wives were included.

The day of the dinner I got very lost in the countryside of Connecticut; this was before cell phones or GPS systems. As I drove around searching, there were no homes for me to borrow a phone. When I finally arrived, I found that they had waited forty-five minutes for me, had given up, and were just starting the first course. I was full of apologies and I could see the relief on their faces that I'd showed up.

I was presented with an inscribed silver mug thanking me for my contributions to Strategic Planning. Being recognized by this special dinner was very touching. To this day I am gratified by the graciousness shown to me.

Reflection: *Looking back, some thirty years later, I am surprised, if not shocked, by the guts, courage, and conviction I displayed. And I am proud of that young Asian American woman in her early forties, speaking out and taking a stand, however naive and idealistic it may have seemed.*

Losing Dad

In 1987, I was living and working in Chicago, as Director, International Business Development, for Telaction, a high-tech start-up. Moving from the New York/Connecticut area to Chicago seemed like a big deal. A few of my friends thought I was moving to the 'middle of nowhere.' Chicago turned out to be a terrific city, with beautiful architecture, a scenic waterfront, and some great restaurants. The winters, though, were downright brutal.

A few years earlier Dad had been diagnosed with kidney failure and put on a dialysis regimen three times a week. The dialysis machine acted as his kidney, filtering and cleaning his blood of the impurities it carried. For younger patients there is the hope and possibility of a kidney transplant, but for someone of Dad's age and deteriorating health, it was not a viable option.

Mom would take him to the hospital in the next town, about twenty-five minutes away, leave him there and go to their motel business to check on the rooms and the maids, then pick Dad up three hours later. She was in her late 60s at the time, and this was quite a taxing schedule for her, on top of daily caring for Dad.

During the years when Dad was ill and also after his passing, Mom kept the motel business going with my brother. She always referred to it as her 'peanut business,' but you could hear the fondness in her tone. It was small, a two-story, twenty-eight unit motel minutes away from Historic Colonial Williamsburg, a popular tourist attraction, especially for families.

In addition to his kidney failure, Dad had other health complications and at different periods in his last years was in and out of hospitals. At times, he was not expected to live past six to twelve months. The fact that Dad lived several years longer than expected by his doctors was truly a gift. Our family was able to have several happy gatherings while Dad was still with us.

Dad had always had a strong fear of hospitals, especially of staying in one. I never knew why, but I sensed it must have been a bad experience in his past. Once I asked, and was allowed, to spend the night with him in his hospital room, which I know comforted him.

There are moments in your life you will always remember. It was October 31, 1987. The phone rang very early in the morning and startled me out of bed. "Is it Dad?" flashed through my sleep-fogged mind. I heard my older sister's tearful voice. "Dinah, we've lost Dad. When can you come?" I burst into tears. It was not totally unexpected, but still, death always comes as a shock. Without a second's thought to my meeting-filled day I said, "I'll come as quickly as I can. I'll take the next flight."

Dad was only 76 when he passed. He'd worked very hard his whole life, ever since he was a young boy growing up on a farm in China. He and Mom had their share of ups and downs; they were very different in temperament and personality. Still, they loved each other deeply and it was clear how much Mom missed him.

After Dad passed away, I realized I'd been so engrossed with my career, with climbing the corporate ladder, that I hadn't seen as much of him in his remaining years as I could have. Yes, I regretted this, and vowed to myself I'd see more of Mom.

During the time I was in the Bush administration in Washington, D.C., 1989-1992, Mom came down with myasthenia gravis, a relatively rare disease that affects various muscles, and she had to be hospitalized at Johns Hopkins in Baltimore,

Maryland. I made sure to visit every few days. When she got home, she could not drive for several months, and I spent every weekend with her to run errands and take her out.

It was in the years after Dad passed that I became much closer to Mom. There's no substitute for spending time with our loved ones. And, there's no more worthwhile way to spend our time.

"A Kinder, Gentler Nation"

In 1989 I was intently focused on climbing the corporate ladder and breaking the "glass ceiling." My plan was to move from Chicago, where I'd been with a high tech start-up, then my own entrepreneurial venture, to New York City. I'd find a great job on Wall Street and finally live in my dream apartment, which I'd bought prior to moving to Chicago. I'd made the purchase before the building was finished, and was able to choose a corner apartment on a high floor with a full view of the Statue of Liberty.

Then, totally unexpectedly, President's Bush's words of "a kinder, gentler nation" awakened in me a long ago dream to serve and give back to my adopted country.

My desire to serve dated back to my high school days. At seventeen, growing up in Ohio, I had a dream of going into the Foreign Service after college. Thus, I spent my freshman year at American University, School of International Service in Washington, D.C. How did it happen for a young Chinese American girl to have such a dream, more than half a century before? I'm not sure. Fate, however, intervened in the form of an early marriage and that dream was not to be.

Ignorance Can Be A Blessing

Looking back, it's a good thing I was totally ignorant about how Washington, D.C.'s political appointee system works. Fortunately, no one sat me down to say, "Look Dinah, you didn't even work in the campaign. You don't stand a chance; forget about getting a job in Washington." I did ask a senior executive acquaintance if he knew anyone. He checked around, then called and said, "Dinah, Washington is flooded with seventy thousand résumés after an election. Without any contacts or connections your chances are pretty slim." He was being tactful. Statistically, my chances were next to zero. Not to be deterred, me, myself and I, the three of us, were convinced the Bush administration needed me, and I could make a contribution.

Never underestimate the power of conviction!

One of my areas of expertise was marketing, and I decided to launch a marketing campaign on my own behalf. I put together a package: reference letters, my official résumé, a personal bio and a compelling cover letter and sent it off by Federal Express. I anxiously awaited a reply. None came, so a few days later I called to make sure someone had received it. I was put on hold as the person asked around, but no one had seen it. I sent off another package, waited, and then called again. And again no one had seen it. Of course my package was buried among the tens of thousands of résumés that flooded the new administration. I sent yet another package and made more follow-up calls. In all I sent off at least four or five FedEx packages, and made dozens of calls. Finally, someone actually got my package.

Never underestimate the power of perseverance!

I wasn't hoping for just any position, I had my ideal position selected—Deputy Assistant Secretary of Services in the Department of Commerce. This was a Senate confirmation level position. Always aim high! Based on my research, this seemed a good fit with my background and experience in high-tech services and finance. My conviction was convincing, and I was able to get interviews with both an Assistant Secretary of Commerce as well as the Undersecretary of Commerce. Both interviews went well, I

Mom and Dad
in their thirties.

Mom and Dad's 50th
Wedding Anniversary.

The Lin children dressed up for Chinese New Years, ca. 1960, (from left) Beth, Ann, Me, Dick.

An impossible childhood dream coming true.

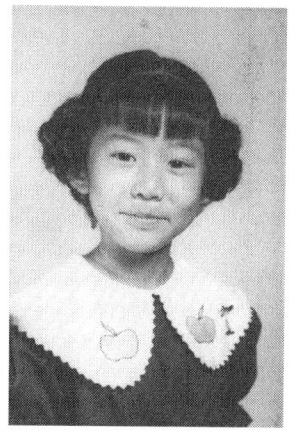

Me, feeling proud of my new perm and new dress.

Christmas at Mom's, ca. 1998.

Christmas in New York with Deb and Jeff, ca. 1988.

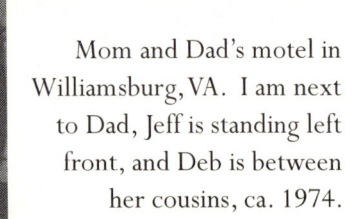

Mom and Dad's motel in Williamsburg, VA. I am next to Dad, Jeff is standing left front, and Deb is between her cousins, ca. 1974.

A wonderful reunion with Deb in Hawaii, 1982.

Corporate years, ca. 1989.

Mom in her red Chinese silk jacket I had tailored made in Beijing.

Getting around the campus.

Sign announcing my talk at Beijing Language and Culture University.

Farewell dinner for a classmate; that's Eagle standing next to me.

One of many speeches while serving in the Bush administration.

Plaque of Appreciation at my farewell reception at the Office of Personnel Management, 1992.

Opening of new Burger King in Seoul, Korea. Mr. Lee, the new franchisee, is on the right.

was hopeful. Then came the final interview, with the political personnel office of the new administration.

She was a middle-aged woman and I can still see the expression on her face and hear the tone of her voice, as she asked me the critical final question, "Who's your angel in the White House?" I gulped. In my ignorance and naiveté, this was a question I never expected. I could only reply, "I don't have an angel in the White House." She lowered her voice, which felt like a pat on the head, and very sympathetically said, "Well, my dear, the other candidates have so-and-so supporting them. Better luck next time."

So much for my Deputy Assistant Secretary position. With no political backing or connection of any kind, I realized it was simply not possible to get a DAS appointment. It's a miracle I received an appointment at all, let alone one at the Senior Executive Service level.

They Hired You On Merit!

Soon after I arrived in Washington in late spring, 1989, there were numerous briefings, receptions, and get togethers for the political appointees. The standard greeting was, "What did you do in the campaign?" People would then launch into their 'war stories' about what they did to help President Bush get elected. I, on the other hand, could only say, "I was busy with my start-up. I didn't work in the campaign." I would get a startled look, often with an opened mouth. It was a conversation stopper. The questioner would be dumbfounded; they'd never heard such a thing. Once, a person blurted out, "My G…they hired you on merit!"

After a few months the interest in what you did in the campaign died down but it invariably would come up sooner or later at gatherings of political appointees. It's possible I was the only senior appointee, or the only appointee, who did not work in the campaign. A distinction of sorts, I guess.

Unbeknownst to me, the news of my appointment spread among the politically active Asian American organizations in the nation's capitol. Soon after my arrival a group of leaders invited me for lunch and I gladly accepted their invitation, unaware of what was in store for me. It soon became clear they expected me to know all the key "players" as they threw names around. They also assumed I had high-level connections, and thus could help advance their particular causes. How else would I have secured a senior appointment?

I felt confused, inadequate, and a bit embarrassed as I stumbled through our conversation. I was a novice on a foreign playing field, not even knowing the rules of the game. Thinking back, I should simply have told them what actually had happened—that my desire to serve and to follow a dream, plus my determination and perseverance, ultimately overcame my lack of connections. This would have surprised, even shocked, these veteran political players, but it would have cleared the air for us to have a more productive discussion.

Reflection: *I am learning it's far better to speak our truth, then to hold back what we're thinking or how we're feeling. I've long had a tendency to hold back, as I don't want to hurt the other person's feelings, or cause tension over differences. It takes courage to speak up—but it's the best course of action.*

Leaving a Legacy

My initial appointment was Associate Director, the number two position, at the Minority Business Development Agency at the Department of Commerce. Ours was a small agency with about forty-five people at the time and only two political appointees, my boss, the Director, and myself. It didn't take long for me to see my boss "playing politics" in the loan approval process, which was directly under my responsibility. He could, and did, override my decisions and approved loans that did not meet the required criteria.

I found myself in an excruciating dilemma. Being a new player in Washington and the administration, I hadn't yet made any close friends, nor was there anyone I could turn to for advice. I wrestled with this for weeks. I finally decided this situation was something I could not live with; it was a matter of my integrity. My best recourse was to quit, and I'd hardly begun.

Before handing in my resignation, I went to see Connie Neuman, the Director of Office of Personnel Management (OPM), the government's top personnel person and a political appointee. I felt I should let someone else, besides my boss, know that I was resigning and the reason, though this had to be stated carefully. OPM is one of three central management agencies of the U.S. federal government; the other two are Office of Management and Budget (OMB) and General Services Administration (GSA).

I tactfully explained my differences with the Director of MBDA, and why I was going to resign. She said, "Dinah, you've got a lot to offer. Don't leave yet; let me see what I can do." She got back to me shortly and offered me a position in her own agency as Director, Office of International Affairs. When my friends heard, they said, "Dinah, you're in marketing and business development. This is personnel. What are you going to do after you leave?" They were implying this was a career stopper.

One of my first actions upon taking office was to issue a memo to the other eighteen Directors of OPM that "we do not secure visas." This was to make clear ours was not a travel office, a function it had taken on under my predecessor. I then set out to redefine and reshape the responsibilities and role of the Office of International Affairs.

OPM was visited by many governments around the world interested in learning how the U.S. federal government operated, and how it managed its hundreds of thousands of employees. OPM received, on average, three to five foreign delegations every week, sometimes two or more in one day. As the Director of International Affairs, I personally welcomed each delegation. I gave them a twenty-minute overview, using three large charts I had created. My overview enabled them to have a clear understanding of the U.S. federal government organizational structure.

Very quickly it became apparent that one of the big problems the Office of International Affairs faced was the quality of briefings from the various OPM departments varied greatly and depended entirely on the person giving the briefing. More often than not, the person I preferred to give the briefing would not be available.

With my marketing experience, I knew how to create quality presentations. I set up meetings with each of the other eighteen Directors to pitch the idea of creating a modular presentation for their department. This would require a commitment of upfront time by some of their staff, but subsequently would save precious time. The benefits were clear: Once the presentations were created, no further preparation time would be needed; different people could give the briefing; visitors would receive a consistent, high quality presentation every time; a much better control of timing was possible; and, importantly, the foreign visitors had hard copies to follow along, which greatly aided their comprehension.

This was a huge task. As an example, when I met with the people from Classifications, they brought out volumes of very thick manuals, and piles of documents, expecting me to go through all of it to select what would be needed for the presentation. They were accustomed to talking from their own knowledge, invariably going on and on, and of course totally losing their audience. I had to meet with them numerous times to extract key information to create a core briefing of forty minutes. We then included additional information to expand the presentation up to two-and-a-half hours. I did this with all eighteen departments, so the briefings were modular and expandable.

Our modular briefings were a huge success. For many of the foreign officials, the Office of Personnel Management was the first, or only, U.S. government agency they visited. This made it all the more important, in my mind, to create a positive impression and experience for them. Once the modular presentations were completed, they worked like a charm. My office would get calls that such-and-such a group wanted to visit OPM. I would fax them our list of eighteen briefing topics and ask that they select those they wanted. Some visitors elected to spend two entire days with us.

****

It was 1989, and the Berlin Wall had fallen. To much of the world, this symbolically represented the end of the Cold War. At last, free market capitalism and the ideals of the Western free nations, led by the United States, had triumphed over centrally (mis) managed economies and the principles of communism.

One of the East European countries that visited OPM was Poland, eager to learn how the U.S. government system was managed and how it operated. The Polish government established an institute to train civil servants. Understandably, the Poles were woefully lacking in experienced and knowledgeable trainers. They asked me for help, and I felt this would be a most worthwhile project. However, they lacked the funds to pay for travel and out-of-pocket expenses, and OPM had no budget item earmarked for this.

Not willing to let this request die, I embarked on a government-wide search for program funding. I visited at least a dozen departments and agencies, including the Departments of Labor, Education, Commerce, Transportation, USAID and, finally, the United Nations Development Programme (UNDP). After meetings with both the Director of UNDP in New York and the local representative, A Memorandum of Understanding was signed between the Office of Personnel Management and UNDP. OPM would provide its senior civil servants for a period of up to one month each, the Polish training institute would provide local room and board, and the UNDP funding would provide the travel and other out-of-pocket expenses. The program enabled OPM to play a valuable role in assisting the Polish government in training its new civil service.

****

There was a third major program of which I am very proud. It was a bold idea, never undertaken before. The program accepted, on a very selective basis, a small number of senior officials from foreign governments. They would spend a month at the Federal Executive Institute, located in Charlottesville, VA. FEI is the premier training institute for senior executives of the U.S. federal civil service. The idea for this program came to me as I saw how interested the foreign officials were in OPM's training programs. I believed this program would be mutually beneficial. The foreign participants, being senior civil servants, would be in a position to spread the knowledge gained when they returned to their own governments. Likewise, U.S. attendees of FEI would benefit from interacting with senior foreign officials.

A great example of this was in 1990, shortly after the Gulf War, when a senior official from a Middle Eastern country was at FEI. It was a wonderful opportunity for increased dialogue between this individual and his counterparts in the U.S. government, leading to greater understanding on both sides.

"The Best of Both Worlds"

In 1989 there were few Asians in the federal government, and even fewer at the senior level. Elaine Chao was Deputy Secretary at the Department of Transportation and the highest ranking Asian-American in government at the time. At the Senior Executive Service level there were only a handful of us. As such, I was often invited to speak, especially during May—Asian Pacific American Heritage month. I welcomed and enjoyed these opportunities of addressing the different departments, agencies and organizations of the federal government.

Unfortunately, I no longer have copies of my speeches from those days. There is, however, one that still stands out in my mind. One day I was mulling over what to say and trying to come up with a title. I knew I wanted to talk a bit about my own background: born in Shanghai, growing up in Ohio, living many years in Asia, and always, since I was a child, imbued with immense pride in being Chinese American. Suddenly, the words came to me—"The Best of

Both Worlds." I knew immediately this was the title of my talk. To this day, these words resonate with me, as I feel the blessings of my dual heritage.

It's hard to believe it's been nearly a quarter of a century since my idealistic, determined self actually managed to achieve the "impossible" dream, securing a senior political appointment at the federal level, not knowing a single person in Washington, D.C.

During my career, I worked for at least a half dozen companies, from high-tech start-ups to Fortune 500 corporations. Most of it was exciting and rewarding, both intellectually and financially. Nonetheless, I would say my three-and-a-half years in government service during the Bush administration were among the most satisfying of my career.

I worked with and met some exceptional people. I learned, first hand, some of the intricacies of our federal government. I enjoyed the international and intellectual culture of our nation's capital. Most importantly, I lived a dream: to serve my adopted country by playing a role, however small, in helping to foster relations and increase understanding between the U.S. and other nations.

A Sandwich Not a Buffet

"They only want a sandwich and you want to give them a buffet," the psychologist said to me. He had been contracted by Burger King to give an array of psychological testing to potential senior hires. The battery of tests which took two days including the feedback, included psychological, intellectual as well as leadership capabilities, among others. I was being interviewed for a corporate-level position, Vice President of Worldwide Business Development.

Truthfully, I was rather amazed to be considered for this position. As with all the positions I held over my corporate career, this position had not been advertised or "open." At the time, few people in the company even knew about this. I believe in Divine Timing! Let me tell you the story behind my initial interview.

I was still in the federal government in Washington, D.C., as Director, Office of International Affairs, at OPM. I had always told myself I would not catch "Beltway fever" and remain on and on in Washington, becoming one of the legions of lobbyists. From the outset, I intended to serve only one term, whether George H.W. Bush ran again or not. Thus, in the summer of 1992 I began keeping an eye open for my next move.

I was walking through the lobby of a five star hotel when a big sign caught my eye. The events board announced a two-day conference being held by Burger King. A few days later I read a lead story in *Forbes* about Burger King's "turnaround" under its charismatic and visionary new Chairman, Barry Gibbs. As I read the article, I felt a mounting enthusiasm about the promising future of this company. The new CEO had laid out an exciting new strategic plan. I thought, "This is the company I'd like to work for." From Human Resources in the government to fast food? I looked at this from the perspective of my interest and experience in the international arena.

Being an action-oriented person I picked up the phone, dialed the company, asked to speak to Mr. Gibbs, and was put through to his secretary. I introduced myself and asked to speak to him. Of course that was not possible. I did, however, manage to convey to her my admiration for her boss, my enthusiasm for the direction he was taking the company, and my interest in exploring opportunities. She gave me the usual "Send in your résumé…" which I always made sure I never did.

After our initial conversation, I made follow-up calls every other week or so, and aways had a pleasant chat with his secretary. One day I told her I needed to make a trip to Miami for another reason (a white lie) and could I stop in at Burger King for even a brief chat with Mr. Gibbs? I was somewhat surprised, but then again not really, when this was arranged, and off I flew from Washington, D.C. to Miami for the day at my own expense.

Burger King's corporate headquarters was an impressive structure with the handful of top senior executives ensconced on the top floor. I stepped off the elevator into this hushed, private sanctum. I don't remember what was discussed with the CEO, but I do know I was well prepared, having done extensive research on the company. After about twenty minutes he said I should meet with his Senior Vice President for Finance to whom the current VP Worldwide Business Development reported. I sat patiently in the waiting area to meet with the SVP, and sat, and sat. I started to worry about missing my flight. Finally, I was called in.

I had flown from Washington, D.C. to Miami at my own expense to meet the Chairman & CEO, for twenty minutes, for the express purpose of making a favorable impression in order to be considered a potential employee. I had no idea, of course, whether there was even an appropriate position available. When I met with the SVP, it turned out that the current VP of Worldwide Business Development was being transferred back to Europe, and there would be an opening in a few months.

My heart jumped! Was he saying I could be considered for this senior position? I had not even dreamed this possibility, to be a VP at the corporate level of a Fortune 500 company. I would undergo an interview process, and other internal and external candidates would be considered, of course. But I felt ecstatic even to be considered. This time, the company paid for my air ticket.

During the interview process no one mentioned China, and neither did I. I sensed China was not even on their radar screen. My predecessor had focused on Europe and I knew my focus would be on Asia, the up-and-coming growth area. I knew the area well, having lived in four countries and Hong Kong over a fifteen-year period, and having traveled there on business.

From the start I felt the position of Vice President Worldwide Business Development should report to the CEO. To me, the international market deserved strategic considerations and a longer term perspective. Unfortunately, Burger King was known for its "revolving door" at the top, for its CEO, EVPs and SVPs. The focus, not surprisingly, was on results in the next twelve and twenty-four months, not years down the road. After a few months on the job I decided to bring China onto the radar screen of my boss, the SVP Finance and other senior executives, including the CEO.

My first trip to China for Burger King was in 1993. There were no direct flights then; all flights were via Hong Kong. I flew first from Miami to Los Angeles, then caught the international flight. Not many people were going to China in those days. After the Tiananmen "incident" in 1989, many foreign businesses pulled out or drastically reduced their presence in China. As I stepped off the plane in Beijing, I was astonished and aghast at the small run-down airport terminal. Huge posters of Mao, Lenin, and Stalin greeted me. The bumpy dirt-like narrow two-lane road into the city had more buses than cars. In the early '90s, China was decidedly very much a developing country.

It's a Can of Worms!

"It's a can of worms. You don't want to touch it with a ten foot pole!" my boss, the CFO, exclaimed when I asked, "What's the story with our franchisee in South Korea?" He went on to say that Burger King's Managing Director, Asia, a Singaporean based in Singapore was working on it, and we (in corporate HQ) did not need to get involved. The managing director in Singapore did not report to my boss, but rather up the chain of command to the Executive Vice President, Asia. Clearly, my boss did not want to have anything to do with what he viewed as a losing proposition.

But I saw a problem here, and a danger to Burger King. Before my time, in the 80s, Burger King was in Hong Kong and the franchisee fell into bankruptcy. Burger King let the business die and effectively exited the market. When a business, especially a consumer business, leaves a market, the people remember that, and it's very difficult to re-enter. Burger King finally re-entered Hong Kong in 2007.

In South Korea, the parent company of the Burger King franchisee was in bankruptcy, and the handwriting was on the wall. Despite my boss's directive to ignore this issue, I followed the situation as closely as I could. I sensed things were deteriorating with no action being taken by either Burger King or the franchisee. In what can only be described as a delicate and carefully maneuvered series of steps—in other words behind my boss's back—I managed to put this situation on the CEO's radar. Importantly, I received his tacit support for me to make a trip to investigate the situation first hand. Thinking back, I'm amazed at my temerity at the time.

Burger King had two Korean nationals on the ground who worked with the managing director in Singapore. The first item on my agenda when I got to Seoul was to visit all six of the Burger King stores. What I saw dismayed and angered me. The storefronts and dining areas were run-down, dirty and messy, and the kitchen was just as bad, or worse. As I went from store to store I could see, at a glance, they were in operational default, not meeting the required standards of maintenance and cleanliness. How had the managing director from Singapore not seen this on his trips to Seoul?

I had scheduled a meeting at my hotel with the franchisee the morning following my visits. I suspected they were trying to find someone to buy the franchise development agreement from them, receive money under the table, then present this party to us as a *fait accompli* as the new franchisee.

After a few sentences of conversation, I got right to the point. I told them what no one at Burger King had been willing to tell them. "I visited all the stores, and they are disgusting! They are clearly in operational default! We,

Burger King, will not allow you to make any private deals for your current Development Agreement." I think I pounded the table. I was indignant and angry, they were ruining our valuable brand!

The two men looked at each other, then at me, stunned. They had never heard a Westerner speak to them so bluntly, let alone a woman, and an Asian American woman at that! I could see they weren't sure what to say. I'd caught them off guard. I then reminded them what was in the contract. I told them Burger King was going to find a new franchisee and sign a new Development Agreement; they could then negotiate with the successful party to take over their existing leases.

I called the managing director in Singapore and told him he and his people needed to get to Seoul right away to undertake a thorough audit of the stores and start the operational default process. This was a very detailed and systematic process, conducted over several months. If the franchisee remained in default after being given several opportunities to correct their non-compliance, then the Development Agreement is declared null and void.

I knew there was no way the franchisee would be able or willing to meet the required standards. This was a process the managing director in Singapore should have initiated months earlier, as the problem had existed for over a year. He didn't like Korea, avoided visiting, and ignored the problem. And it seemed his boss and corporate HQ had chosen to ignore the problem as well.

The other piece of my strategy was to pay a visit to the Ministry of Health. This was to preempt the possibility the franchisee would file a complaint to the government, maintaining that they were being unfairly treated by a big American corporation, out to take advantage of them. And of course the new Agreement with a new franchisee would need government approval. I paid a courtesy visit to a senior official to give him a "heads up" on the situation and the steps we were were taking vis-a-vie the current franchisee. Being a well-know international brand in Korea in the early 90s, Burger King had visibility and consumer recognition. I did not want the brand image to suffer bad publicity.

The senior official I met with was polite and seemed appreciative of my visit. I stated the facts of the situation and told him my plan for rescuing the business. He knew it was far preferable for a visible international brand to succeed than to fail and reflect negatively on doing business in Korea.

It was fortunate Burger King had an experienced young Korean lady, Miss Kim, in her 30s, who spoke very good English. For my trips to Seoul she was my interpreter, driver, executive assistant, and sounding board. Burger King also had the services of a good law firm, an absolute necessity for doing business in a foreign country. I spent hours going over all the documentation, including all the filings, for the

Burger King business in Korea. And a good thing I did. We discovered an omission which, had it not been rectified, could have prevented Burger King from successfully installing a new franchisee.

As for the managing director from Singapore, he made the minimum number of trips to Seoul, stayed the minimum amount of time, and then hightailed it back to Singapore. The Koreans were known to be "rough and tumble" business people, and he admitted fearing for his safety.

There were two major processes going on simultaneously. On one hand, steps needed to be taken to put the current franchisee into operational default in order to terminate the Development Agreement. At the same time, I needed to look for a new franchisee. Once we let the word out, there were a number of interested parties. Of course this was all new to me, and there was no one available, either at HQ or on the ground, I could turn to for advice.

As usual, I relied on my own analytical thinking and creative intuition.

After evaluating the half dozen or so proposals, I decided I'd meet with the top three. One of the three was Mr. Lee, who came with his American consultant, Harry. It turns out Mr. Lee had an MBA from New York University and spoke excellent English. What impressed me most was that Mr. Lee was the Korean licensee for Perry Ellis and Guess.

As soon as I walked into his stores, I could tell this was a person with discriminating taste and marketing savvy.

His stores were simply a cut above the rest. In retailing (in those pre-Internet days) it was all about location, location, location. Mr Lee had a full-time real estate team, scouting the best locations.

I'd found my ideal franchisee!

Then, came the hard part—negotiating the Development Agreement. Thinking back, this was the part where I needed the input and help of more experienced hands, and I didn't have it. In fact, I had scant support from my direct boss, who had told me it was a can of worms and, grudging, slow support from our legal department, always overloaded with work. Thankfully, I knew I had the tacit and moral support of the CEO, which encouraged me in my efforts to rescue the business.

An Unforgettable New Year's Eve

There are some holidays you never forget. They are memorable, though the memory may be pleasant or painful, sometimes both. For nearly a year I had worked on rescuing Burger King's business in South Korea, successfully taking back our Development Agreement from a bankrupt franchisee and finding an ideal new franchisee to take over the business. Now we were down to the nitty-gritty details of the Development Agreement—details such as the schedule for the opening of new stores and, importantly, the upfront fee to be paid as well as the royalty on sales.

A lot had been accomplished and, ideally, we would reach an agreement early the next year. But my boss, the SVP Finance, wanted to book the sizable upfront fee as income for the current year. To achieve this, I had no choice but to have a face-to-face negotiation session before the end of the year. At all the meetings with me, Mr. Lee had his American consultant with him, and I was always alone. From a negotiation perspective, it would have been a psychological advantage had I had another person on my side of the table, even if the person did nothing but sit there. Fortunately, I managed to hold my own quite well.

It was December 31, 1993, New Year's Eve day in the States and New Year's Eve evening in Korea. We were meeting in a conference room at my hotel. The air was tense, and we needed to take several breaks. I was at a psychological disadvantage; they knew I very much wanted a signed agreement before midnight. At one point I had to call my boss. He still wanted to play hardball, and the clock was against us! Fortunately, I had a mutually respectful and cordial relationship with Mr. Lee and especially with Harry, and this was key.

Finally, at 11:45 p.m. Korean time, we reached an agreement. Mr. Lee signed and I signed, then I called my boss with the good news. Both sides were exhausted. I even forgot about champagne! It was, indeed, a New Year's Eve to remember.

Reflection: *In a way, I've never given myself credit for whatever I've achieved. I just take it all in stride, expecting nothing less from myself. While this can be admirable in a way, it also takes away from allowing myself to feel pride and a sense of accomplishment for what I've done. I've since come to believe it's important to acknowledge and celebrate myself, and my wins, though sometimes I still forget.*

Three months later Mr. Lee opened several new stores. Ever the consummate marketer, he had traveled to the U.S. and picked up a collection of 50s memorabilia for his three themes: American movies, sports, and music. He obtained the pre-approval of Burger King to have these design departures from the template. Not surprisingly, customers loved these exciting, innovative Burger Kings and business started to boom. Burger King franchisees from other countries including those in the U.S. heard about Mr. Lee's stores and traveled to Seoul to see them and get ideas.

Reflection: *Once, on one of my Asian trips I was talking with another international executive on the plane and mentioned the problem Burger King had had in Korea. He was astounded I'd been able to resolve the complex issue within a year, saying* *that, in his experience, in Korea, a problem such as the one I'd faced would normally have taken at least two years to resolve. Of course I hadn't known that and had proceeded at my usual pace. And of course my boss, having never traveled to Asia, had little appreciation for this fact.*

Putting China On the Radar Screen

I joined Burger King in October 1992. China was not mentioned by anyone and I wisely didn't mention it in the beginning. However, China was definitely on my radar screen from day one and I very carefully laid the groundwork to put it on the CEO's radar screen as well. Over a period of months I engaged in subtle lobbying through memos of my exploratory trips and multiple brief conversations. At last, I managed to convince our CEO and our EVP Marketing to take a week out of their tightly packed schedules to make a trip to China, to see the vast potential of this market with their own eyes.

I felt our CEO and EVP only needed to see the crowds in McDonald's—practically 24/7—to know there was growing consumer acceptance of the hamburger, heretofore a strange food to the Chinese. I was amazed at seeing people eating at McDonald's early in the morning, and seeing grandparents there, happy to splurge on their only grand child. With the one child policy it meant every child had four grandparents for whom he or she was the only grandchild.

Once I put the word out that Burger King was looking at potentially entering China, there was no shortage of interested parties. Most did not meet my requirements. I soon realized no one party would have all the credentials: substantial financial backing, direct operating experience, and the critically needed 'guan xi' (relationship) with the local/provincial governments. By definition, the latter had to be a local entity. If the interested party were a Beijing-based company, they would not have the needed connections and contacts in Shanghai and vice versa. In fact, being a Shanghainese operating in Beijing or vice versa could be a distinct disadvantage. The Chinese put a lot of importance on provincial ties, unlike the U.S. where it hardly matters what state you're from. Not surprisingly, there were no Chinese companies with the necessary operating experience, since fast food western style was a new concept in China at that time.

I spent many hours debating with my boss, the SVP Finance. Unbelievably to me, he wanted to grant a franchise to just one entity for all of China. He was going by the model of the other countries in Asia and Europe, where this was being done. I couldn't seem to convince him that to do so in a country the size of China would be tantamount to having only one franchisee for all of the U.S.

My ideal scenario was to have the "money party" be a Hong Kong-based entity, the operating party be someone like the Sun brothers who were the initial franchisee for McDonald's in Taiwan, and then a powerful local entity who could cut through the red tape for all the myriad government approvals and permits. I also thought the best would be to have three strong franchisees to start, one in the north in Beijing, another one midway down the eastern coast in Shanghai, and a third in the south, Guangzhou.

To help with this process, I hired a U.S.-based China consulting firm. The person assigned to our account was fluent in Chinese which, at the time, I was not. This was a necessity for the meetings held in China where no English was spoken. Over the course of nine months a number of meetings were held in Hong Kong, Shanghai, Beijing, Taipei and Los Angeles.

Reflection: *Over the course of my career in the corporate world, I held dozens of meetings with potential clients/customers/ franchisees in Asia, always all men, usually at least two of them, and sometimes a conference table full. Only once do I remember another woman in a meeting. Yes, I was very much (alone) in a man's world! Now thinking back, I'm amazed I don't remember feeling intimidated or at a disadvantage. In fact, I didn't think about it at all. There was a job to do, and it was up to me to do it! Once, I made an overseas trip on crutches, and was in quite* *a bit of pain when sitting for long periods, which I certainly did on the long flights, and, in long meetings.*

McDonald's at Tiananmen Square

The brightly lit structure at the corner of Tiananmen, the wide boulevard that runs in front of the Imperial Palace, shone like a beacon, the only illumination in sight, surrounded by darkness. This was 1993, and I was standing in front of McDonald's flagship store in Beijing. It stood on an exceptionally coveted location, a mere block from Tiananmen Square and the Imperial Palace, a prime tourist spot for foreigners and Chinese alike. It no longer occupies that corner spot, it had to make way for Hong Kong billionaire Li Ka-shing's multi-million dollar Oriental Plaza development. Whatever leverage or 'guan xi' McDonald's had in order to secure the location in the first place, it was no match for that of Mr. Li.

In those days, and for many years afterwards, the Chinese were not used to standing in a queue. Wherever you went, there would be a crunch of people all squeezed, or trying to squeeze, at the counter, and it would be sheer bedlam. This was as true at the bank as it was at McDonald's. If you didn't want to squeeze, you simply never got your money or your food! It's amazing that somehow this 'system,' or lack thereof, managed to work for hundreds of years.

Back then, there were only four McDonald's in Beijing and mere dozens of Kentucky Fried Chicken outlets. On my trips I would always visit a number of stores. I felt it was my duty, though not my pleasure, to sample the burgers and fries and fried chicken. One cannot overestimate what a feat it was in those days to duplicate the taste of the food to that served by franchisees in the U.S. Also, to achieve consistent quality, not only in the food but in the cleanliness of the stores and bathrooms. Clean bathrooms have always been high on my list, and speak to me of the management of a place. It's as true here in the U.S. today, as it is in China or anywhere else.

Always strategic in their approach, McDonald's had been cooperating for years with both the U.S. Department of Agriculture and the Chinese Ministry of Agriculture, experimenting with different potato hybrids before they actually opened their first store. They were trying to replicate not only the taste and consistency, but also the size of the potato, to get the nice, long fries that American consumers had loved for so long. It sounds odd to say, but the greatest operating challenge facing McDonald's was being able to grow the ideal potato they needed to produce the perfect French fry. This speaks to one of their secrets to success and their ability to achieve worldwide dominance.

China Postscript

Entering any new market, but especially the China market, and especially in the early 90s, required long-term strategic vision and ample resources, especially the manpower to support an entry and, afterwards, its subsequent growth. At the time, Burger King had neither. Personally, I felt gratified to have put China on the radar screen of our CEO, for him to even have considered the possibility of a pilot project in China. It would be a decade before Burger King finally did enter the China market with a few stores in Shanghai, and, after that, with a single store at the new Beijing airport.

Leaving Corporate America

At the time, I didn't consciously have this thought, but by becoming a corporate-level vice president at a Fortune 500 company I had, in my mind, broken "the glass ceiling." Perhaps subconsciously I heaved a sigh of relief and said to myself, "At last!" It had only been sixteen years from the time I'd started in my first full-time job, as an entry-level analyst at Chase Manhattan in Hong Kong, not bad progress, if I say so myself. But, characteristically, I didn't pat myself on the back, celebrate, or give it a second thought.

Weeks before the company made the official announcement, there were whispers in the halls that a major "reorganization" was underway. We all knew what this meant. Jobs would be cut. This news was certainly unexpected, to me and to most of the employees. Anyone who's ever gone through this experience knows it's very unsettling, not knowing whether you'd have a job the next day.

I'd never been risk adverse, having joined several high tech start-ups, where you know the chances for success are slim. Still, this time, I'd hoped and expected to be with the company longer, maybe even until retirement. After my Korea success, I felt I was on a roll, and ready to look for a new franchisee for a re-entry into the Hong Kong market. I was not ready to leave.

In addition to myself, there were half a dozen other women at the corporate VP level and sometimes we'd have lunch together in the company cafeteria. The conversation would inevitably turn to the re-organization. We conjectured that at least a few of us would survive the cuts. As we nervously looked around, we felt like we were playing musical chairs. As VP, Worldwide Business Development, I knew my position would be a target, as new market entries were not a priority.

In my final weeks at Burger King, I decided I'd walk with my head held high, I would not show defeat or my disappointment. Years earlier I had read somewhere, "Act like a winner when you lose." I thought that was wise advice, which I tried to remember.

At the time I left Burger King, I felt I needed a break from "Corporate America." I don't know if I was "burned out," but I had certainly pushed myself, mentally and physically, and there had been an emotional toll as well. Being good, even very good, at your job does not mean it feels emotionally satisfying. I'd always been entrepreneurial and being in a large corporation was not a natural fit. I valued freedom and flexibility over security and structure.

Instead of truly taking some time off, just to rest and recharge, I jumped right into an entrepreneurial venture. I started out with enthusiasm, but the venture was bound to fail, as my heart wasn't in it. This wasn't the first time I'd responded to unemployment by immediately jumping into a new venture, as if "downtime" was a dirty word and something to be avoided. The irony is that "downtime" was just what I needed; downtime could have allowed me the space and silence to hear my wise inner guidance.

Reflection: *Looking back, I was something of a 'slave driver' with myself, and rather hard on others as well. Whether I was flying to Europe or Asia, I would arrive the day or evening before my meeting, then hit the deck running the next day for a packed week of meetings and appointments, and fly back on the weekend. I'd have Sunday to unpack and get ready for the week, then be back in the office first* *thing Monday. Could I have given myself an extra day on each end to rest? Could I have taken a few vacation days to see the countryside or to just "play," especially in London, Paris and Milan? Looking back, I really do wish I'd been easier on myself in my hectic climb up the corporate ladder. I also wish I'd taken more time for friends. Friendship takes time, and I didn't have the time, so I told myself. Once, I told a friend the ideal relationship for me would be if the man lived in a different state, and we'd see each other every other weekend. She said, "Dinah, what man would want that?" Turns out she was right!*

Following A Dream Back Home

And most important, have the courage to follow your heart and intuition.
- Steve Jobs

China 1973

The seeds of my desire to learn Chinese date back to 1973, one year after Nixon's historic visit began the opening of China to the West. We were living in Hong Kong at the time, due to my husband's job. We had a group of Chinese friends, all of whom had been educated abroad, either in the U.S. or Europe. Someone in the group had connections with officials in China and offered the opportunity for a group of us to make a trip to the Mainland. In 1973, this was unheard of. Individuals had gone in, but no groups. China had been closed to the outside world for nearly a quarter century, this was an exciting opportunity!

There were nineteen of us, mostly young couples and a few singles, all under the age of forty. The women were told to dress conservatively, in pants, no skirts. I don't remember if anything was said about makeup, but we all kept that to a minimum. The idea was not to stand out, though that proved to be impossible. As much as we downplayed our appearance, we still stood out like beacons. We were constantly stared at and people gathered wherever we went. I had a taste of what it must feel like to be a celebrity. Huge crowds would congregate outside our hotel, especially in the mornings, waiting for us to appear. The crowds were quiet and respectful but it was still somewhat daunting to be stared at for nineteen days. We were the only "foreigners" they'd ever seen, though we were all Chinese by race.

To look out into the crowd was to look at a sea of grey. At that time, everyone in China, male and female, wore either grey or navy. The unisex attire was the loose-fitting 'Mao jacket' with baggy trousers. All the women had their hair cut bluntly below the ear. Young girls all wore pigtails. Keep in mind this was 1973. China was a very poor country back then and scarce resources had to be utilized for other things, not attire or personal appearance. Further, this was part of the mandated egalitarianism. Occasionally you saw a young child wearing a bit of color, and it would be such a cheerful sight, popping out in the sea of grey.

Every detail of our nineteen-day visit was closely orchestrated and supervised. We had no say in where we went, what we saw, or what we did. We entered China via Macao, then still a Portuguese colony. We were required to leave our passports there, and were issued traveling papers. Throughout our nineteen days, there were many checkpoints where we had to show our Chinese papers. Each time I could feel palpable tension in the air, as if at any moment something could go wrong and we'd be detained. In fact, I had a feeling of apprehension and trepidation that never left me the whole time I was there. I don't know why, as we were legally in China and there was no danger, but the air itself seemed oppressive to me. When we returned to Macao and got our passports back, our whole group heaved a sigh of relief.

We visited nine cities in nineteen days: Beijing, Shanghai, Tianjin, Hangzhou, Suzhou, Wuxi, Nanjing, Guangzhou and Xian. We were amazed and enchanted by the natural beauty of the country and the various charming sights. It seemed there was never quite enough time for the sights, as our schedule was filled with schools and factories.

The scenario was the same every place we visited. We'd be ushered into a room, where we'd sit around the perimeter while we were served tea. A committee of three would greet us and the presentation would begin. First we'd hear about the history of the place, then all the obligatory facts about the 'liberation' (they still refer to 1949 and the establishment of the People's Republic of China this way). The talk would drone on for at least forty-five minutes, often longer. Most in our group knew only Cantonese, a very different dialect than Mandarin but could partially understand. Some of us knew little or no Mandarin but tried our best to look interested nonetheless.

The factories we toured were, quite simply, pathetic. The buildings were sad and run down and the machinery was woefully outdated. Nonetheless, the Chinese proudly showed them off, totally ignorant of how behind China was at that time.

We longed to see the 'real face' of China, not only what the officials wanted us to see, but this was wishful thinking, as it was quite impossible to wander off. We were under close supervision every minute. We may not have liked being supervised so closely, but I can understand their thinking.

To my knowledge, we were the first 'foreign' group to be allowed into China for a tour of the country. Everyone in our group was Chinese by birth, born either on the Mainland, in Taiwan or in Hong Kong. The Chinese were anxious to create the best possible impression, knowing we would talk about our visit with family, friends, business associates and others. The last thing they wanted was for any mishap to happen to any of us.

Some in the group were able to visit with their relatives and allowed to bring them gifts, all arranged ahead of time, of course. For all of us, this was a memorable trip. I had mixed emotions of pride and pity—pride that China was making progress and had come a long way from periods of internal strife and starvation, and pity for how poor and behind the times the country and the people were.

It's hard to imagine that was only forty years ago. Economic miracle is not too strong a term for those of us who witnessed first hand what the country had been, and what it is now. I don't think even the most optimistic visionary could have foreseen where China would be today. Even in the early-mid 1990s when I traveled there, my main concern about doing business was the "political risk." Would China revert to a 'closed door' policy? The answer then was far from clear.

The seeds of my desire to speak Chinese were planted during that trip in 1973, though it would be more than twenty-five years later before I followed a dream to move to China, study Chinese, and re-connect with my roots.

Crisis = Wei Ji

Over the years I had accumulated a small portfolio of stocks. Most of the time I was too busy to pay much attention, but my modest portfolio seemed to be doing OK. Every now and then a financial advisor would point out that I was overweighted in one particular stock. This was a company I'd worked for in the mid 80s. In fact I had reported directly to the Chairman & CEO and I had faith in the management of the company, which grew rapidly from acquisitions and stock splits. Over the years I continued to add to my position until I had over six figures invested in this one stock.

One day I woke up to discover the stock had fallen to half its value! There had been news of "accounting irregularities." The stock had been the darling of Wall Street and widely held by institutions and funds. Billions were lost overnight. The aftermath of this scandal continued for years. I felt panicked and devastated.

Losing half my life savings and investments overnight was a personal financial crisis. Without a job and living in my sister's basement, I was at a low.

Serendipitously a direct mail piece arrived, trumpeting a free Wade Cook seminar on stock trading, promising an opportunity. Somewhat warily, I decided to go. To my amazement, there were several hundred people at this seminar. The enthusiasm was high as Wade Cook and various speakers told stories of how they'd made their fortunes trading options. I had previously heard of options, but had never understood how they worked. It sounded like an easy way to make money quickly. That should have rung a danger bell! But at the end of the free seminar, I signed up for the course, which included weekend workshops across the country with a "guarantee" that we'd become knowledgeable option traders.

Not only did I want to make back my lost investment which had crashed to half its value, I wanted to make some extra money so I could go live in China and study Chinese. Money had never been a strong motivator for me up until then, but now I needed to make some money, and the quicker the better.

The workshops proved to be more motivational than informative. You know the old saying, *A little knowledge is a dangerous thing*. I learned just enough for it to be dangerous to my financial health! This was the late 1990s, the era of the frothy tech bubble. Unknown companies skyrocketed into the stratosphere, and most crashed back to earth. Fortunes were made and lost.

I moved out of my sister's basement (after she disinvited me) to Fountain Hills, a picturesque town next to Scottsdale, Arizona, on the edge of the Indian reservation. A key factor for choosing Arizona was the decidedly lower cost of living than Connecticut. For the next two years I was totally immersed in my new 'job', trading options. It quickly became an addiction.

Down On My Knees

I was down on my knees, forehead to the floor, hands clasped in prayer. I pleaded, "Please God, tell me what I should do next!" Panic, fear, despair, and desperation engulfed me.

For months I'd been hoping to turn my growing losses in the stock market around. This was 2000, and the tech bubble had burst. I could say I was one of the lucky ones; I did not have a house to mortgage and had not borrowed, but my trading had forced me to liquidate both my retirement accounts, wiping out my life's savings.

How had this happened to me?

I had an MBA in finance, a successful career in the corporate world, and had prepared for my latest venture by taking classes in trading stocks and options. Ah, yes—I learned just enough to be dangerous to myself! I was buying and selling options with names like "naked calls," "naked puts," and "butterfly spreads." Thinking about it now I can only claim temporary insanity.

My objective had been simple: I merely wanted to make back the money I had lost and make some extra money so I could follow my dream to go live in China, study Chinese and reconnect with my roots. I had no idea what a slippery slope I was on. Trading options eventually left me with just ten percent of my life's savings, barely enough for twelve months of living expenses, living frugally.

Beneath my feelings of panic and fear, I felt immense sadness and sorrow as well as shame. I had let myself down. I had failed, big time! I was accustomed to success and winning, not failure and losing. Not since my divorce two decades earlier had I felt such pain and such a sense of failure.

There were lessons for me in this experience, and humility was a big one.

Going to Beijing!

I can see the moment so clearly. My mom and I were standing in her kitchen in the house she and my dad had built in Williamsburg, Virginia. I had meant to break the news to her gently, but I blurted out, "Mom, I've given this a lot of thought, and what I really want to do is to go to China to study Chinese."

Silence.

She looked at me, and in her own caring way, said, "Dinah, at your age? Forget about it!"

I was fifty-eight at the time.

Knowing Mom, I knew she meant well. She pictured me moving halfway around the world to a place where I didn't know a soul. She knew how hard it would be to learn the language. And she knew my financial situation was precarious.

In the weeks leading to my decision, my left brain, stuck in survival mode, had shouted, "Dinah, get a job! Any job!"

But each time my heart whispered, "I still want to go to China…"

How had I, in dire financial straits, decided to go to China anyway? I prayed for guidance and my prayers were answered. I felt I could always get some kind of work, simply being a native English speaker. I also felt it would be easier to live on a shoestring budget in China than in the U.S.

In the end, I listened to my heart and went.

Xijiao Hotel and Global Village

It'd been three years since I'd last been in Beijing and I didn't know what to expect.

I was staying at the Xijiao Hotel on the outskirts of Beijing in the university district. When my mini taxi stopped in front of the new reception building, I thought, "This can't be right!" Feeling puzzled and amazed, I walked through the gleaming revolving doors into a huge open reception area with marble floors, granite counters, and an enormous crystal chandelier that hung from the high ceiling. To appreciate the contrast to the old reception building, imagine the size, look, and feel of a small-town motel front desk versus the lobby of the Waldorf Astoria in New York City, and you'll get an idea.

I did not realize it then, but this was the tip of the iceberg—an indication of the sheer magnitude of transformation that was about to take place in Beijing, and in China, in the coming decade. Truly a quantum leap!

Since I'd last been in Beijing there'd been a growing flood of foreign students wanting to study Chinese. A Korean entrepreneur saw a need and opened a school called Global Village. Fifty-minute classes were continuously taught from 8:00 a.m. to 8:00 p.m. You could choose classes to suit your level and schedule. Such a welcome contrast to the usual rigid university system and program. Students flocked to the Global Village.

The school was housed in an old three-story structure with no heat or air conditioning to speak of. It was so cramped I could barely squeeze down the hall or on the stairs between classes. I'm sure it did not meet fire codes of any kind, but neither did many buildings in those days. Likely no one even noticed or was bothered by this. If you were, you would not have been in China, or studying Chinese.

I was often asked by both Chinese and foreigners why I was studying Chinese. My reply would invariably be, "Because it's my heart's desire. I love learning to speak Chinese." The questioner often looked puzzled, as they expected my reason to be more practical such as "It's for my work," or "So I can do business in China." They couldn't relate to moving halfway around the world, leaving family and friends, to follow a dream.

Best Deal in Beijing

Given my scarce financial resources, I put myself on a strict student budget and ate my lunches and dinners at one of two student cafeterias. The second-floor cafeteria near the Xijiao was a huge open space with row upon row of bench tables. The first time I ate there, I went at peak mealtime and could hardly find a seat. Unlike the university cafeteria, this one housed dozens of small private vendors. The popular vendors always had a crowd of students. Sometimes you had to get pushy to get your food.

This cafeteria was not restricted to students, and there would be workers and people living in the vicinity there as well. Back in those days it was perfectly acceptable to spit chicken bones, or anything else, right on the floor. I learned to watch my step! In winter I ate with my coat on because it was freezing, literally.

Despite the unappealing conditions, there was great variety and the food was tasty. And for only US $0.65 I could get rice and two dishes. Definitely the best deal in Beijing.

New Oriental School

Finding work was very much on my mind. Soon after I arrived I learned from another foreign student about her part-time job at the New Oriental School. I immediately went there to look for Eagle, who was in charge of the oral exam program.

When I found her, Eagle said, "I'll give you a try and if you work out, I'll add your name to my list of teachers." I liked this direct, no-nonsense young lady right away. The teachers were all native English speakers, and our job was to give mock oral exams to students preparing to study in Australia, England, and other European countries that required the International English Language Testing System (IELTS) oral exam.

There were usually four to six of us giving the exams at the same time. We tested four students per hour and sometimes worked eight to ten hour shifts on weekends. To be good at this, we needed to stay alert and focused, student after student. The locations for these exams were always at outlying satellite schools, and getting there took forty-five to sixty minutes in a small van.

The exam room was often a student's dorm room. A small desk would be squeezed between the bunk beds, with the student sitting opposite me. There was no heat or air conditioning. In winter I'd wear leggings under my wool pants, two pairs of socks, and layered sweaters under my down coat, which I'd keep on. Unfortunately I had to take my gloves off to write. In summer I'd be perspiring in the sweltering humidity and heat.

It sounds harsh, even now, as I write this. But at the time it didn't feel harsh. This was simply part of my new life and new reality as a student in China. And I was very glad to have a steady income. We were paid between Renminbi (RMB) 80 and 110 (approximately $10 - $14) per hour. I was soon the highest paid and received the nicest gift at Christmas. One year I was given a gift box of Starbucks coffee and a mug. It's still my favorite coffee mug.

Reflection: *A life-long tendency I've had is to not give myself due credit for my accomplishments. My daughter remarked on this once, saying, "Mom, you simply take your achievements for granted, you never give yourself any credit." One attribute I have given myself credit for, however, is my adaptability. Seemingly overnight I've had* *great changes in my "fortune"— in my outer living circumstances and conditions—and I've accepted these as part of a life of challenge and change. As I've said, adaptability is a great life skill.*

> Journal entry: February 19, 2001
> *I do feel I have been trusting the process of life…overcoming, for the most part, my fear of financial lack. Somehow, Spirit will provide…*

I enjoyed my brief interactions with these students from all over China. From their answers I learned much about their lives. It was heartbreaking to hear how many hated their major in college, which was forced on them by their university or their parents. They seemed too young to be feeling that their lives were beyond their control.

> Journal entry: December 22, 2002
> *I realize I can do without so many of the material goods I once had—and still live a perfectly comfortable life.*

Payday was every other week, and Eagle would meet us one by one in a room and count out our pay in RMB 100 bills. It was such a great feeling holding my wad of RMB 100 notes. After a while, between this job and another one, I was able to pay most of my living expenses. Occasionally, I splurged with a friend at TGIF for chicken salad and a glass of wine for RMB 100. Remember, my cafeteria meals only cost me RMB 4-5.

Which Do You Love More?

When I left for Beijing in September of 2000, I purposely did not set a time for my return. Contrary to the way I'd lived my life all those years in the corporate world, I wanted to simply "go with the flow" and be guided by my intuition, not my analytical left brain. As I neared the end of my first year, there was no question in my mind or heart that I would continue my studies. My Chinese was steadily improving and I was enjoying my new adventure.

Thankfully, my mom and children understood and were supportive. Mom was in fairly good health and had my brother and his family living nearby. My son was establishing his career in southern California, and my daughter was married and living in Hong Kong at the time.

> Journal entry: May 14, 2001
> *I am so grateful and blessed to have good friends here…I feel very blessed to be here.*

My focus remained on studying Chinese and working as many hours as New Oriental School needed me. Partly to earn extra money, I created a talk that I felt would be helpful for the students as they were preparing to study abroad. My talk was titled "Cross Cultural Communication: Perspectives of a Chinese American," pointing out the communication and cultural differences between China and western countries. The student assemblies ranged between 500-900 students. My favorite part was the Q&A.

At my first talk the question came up, "Which do you love more, China or America?" Without hesitation I replied, "Which do you love more, your mom or your dad?" It was the perfect answer. All the students could relate. I went on to say China is like the mother. In fact, China is often referred to as the "Motherland." The U.S. is, of course, "Uncle Sam." I concluded, "I have always considered myself so fortunate to be both Chinese and American."

Journal entry: October 6, 2002
There are many questions about my future — sometimes I haven't a clue what the future holds — I'm learning to be comfortable with that — just trusting in Spirit to guide and provide.

The SARS Scare

It started out as just another piece of news—some kind of rare bird flu, with a very long name, Severe Acute Respiratory Syndrome or SARS. This was February 2003, and the article told of SARS causing a death in southern China. A couple of days later, I saw another article, a few more people had died from this flu. It was beginning to sound a bit worrisome. It seems the news about this strange sounding flu had reached the international media before it reached those of us living in China. I received an email from my son in the States, sounding worried; he had heard about ten people had died from it.

By March, the Chinese media was still reporting it was contained in southern China. But one thing you know about the media in China—it's controlled by the government. I was getting more news from the New York Times online than from local or domestic sources. People were starting to wear face masks on public transportation, which carried stickers with a date to show it had been sprayed with disinfectant that day. Perhaps good for public relations, but I'm not sure how much actual good it did.

By early April, we learned cases of SARS had been discovered in Beijing. As the truth of the severity of the outbreak became known, people started to get really worried as it was much worse than had originally been reported. Officials had shifted hundreds of SARS patients from hospitals to other locations when the World Health Organization was in Beijing, carrying out an investigation. The Minister of Health and the mayor of Beijing were both sacked for the cover-up.

By late April, I could feel mild panic in the air. Schools and universities were closing, for an indefinite period. My Chinese classes were cancelled. People were told by the government to stay home. The May 1 holiday (equivalent to our Labor Day) was cancelled to cut down on travel.

Among my foreign friends, more and more were starting to leave Beijing to go home. I was scheduled to go back to the States for a visit in June. My family was suggesting I come back early. They told me of planeloads of Chinese tourists being turned away by countries frightened of importing the virus, and were worried I'd be quarantined upon arrival from Beijing. The other concern was simply getting out of Beijing at all if a full-blown panic ensued.

By late April, huge and crowded Beijing seemed eerily like a ghost town. Once, I was the lone person on a bus, normally crammed with standing-room-only passengers. The grocery store was packed as everyone stocking was up. My Chinese friends said they were preparing for two months' siege. The cashier at the register asked, "Why don't you have a face mask on?" Nearly everyone in the store had one on. I had read that face masks needed to have multiple layers to have any effect and I found them to be uncomfortable in the warm and humid weather.

At first, I felt I would stick to my original departure date of June. But each day the news seemed to grow worse and there was undeniably a growing feeling of panic. Rumors abounded, including rumors of the city closing down. In the midst of all this, with no way of knowing how much worse it would get, I decided to leave by the end of April.

> Email, April 24, 2003:
> *"The government went from under reporting to what I think now is over reporting. There are so many programs dealing with various aspects of SARS…from how to wash your hands properly to interviewing recovered patients to psychologists telling people there's no need to panic. The TV is giving stats by province: number of cases, number of patients who recovered, and the number of patients who died. You know how it gets, rumors start going around about the city getting sealed off, stopping of transportation etc. What I do know is that a centralized government can do whatever it decides, no dithering around with public opinion or opposition."*

This is, of course, both for better and worse.

During the height of the SARS scare, from the end of April to the end of June 2003, the five-star hotels were down to 5%-10% occupancy, as tourists and business people cancelled their trips. Months later, those hardy souls who chose to stick it out and not leave would tell of being able to get from one end of the city to the other in a record twenty minutes, instead of the usual one-and-a-half hours.

I think the government learned a big lesson from the way they tried to handle SARS in the media. The cover-up backfired in a big way, not only with the international media and public opinion, but with the Chinese people.

By the time I returned to Beijing in July, life was back to normal, and SARS was almost a memory, in a city that moves faster than New York. Back to normal meant the usual gridlock, except now even worse, as people had rushed out to buy cars during SARS, to avoid public transportation.

Heaven and Earth Change Places

By my third year, I was becoming less intense about studying, simply enjoying being able to communicate fluently. About this time I started to do some consulting work. By 2004, I was ready to move. My physical move marked the end of my life as a student and the beginning of my life as a consultant, interacting with the business community.

The government's policy in early 2000 of allowing the Chinese to purchase their own homes set off the beginning of a housing boom that dramatically changed people's lives. The magnitude of change is hard to comprehend.

Over a span of five years, I was invited by a couple who were university professors to visit them in their three different apartments. Very literally, they went from "hovel to heaven," from cement floors to wooden floors, from no kitchen to a kitchen with all modern appliances. Multiply this by millions of people moving and you'd get an idea of the changes transforming China. Once people owned their own homes, they went on a never-ending shopping spree!

When I arrived in China in 2000, there were very few cars and fewer yet that were privately owned. Suddenly, it seemed everyone had a car and traffic jams became the new reality!

By the mid-2000s Beijing was pulling out all the stops for its debut on the world stage as host of the 2008 Olympics. The city seemed to be one enormous construction site! Once, standing in front of my apartment in downtown Beijing, I counted seventeen multi-story cranes in the skyline.

The Olympics allowed the world to see a new China emerging, one much stronger economically, more confident, proud of its achievements, and ready and willing to play a larger role on the world stage.

The Chinese have a proverb: "Tian Fan Di Fu" which, literally translated, means "Heaven and Earth change places." This is an apt phrase to describe the unprecedented transformation of China in the decade 2000-2010.

If anyone had suggested to me at the outset of my Chinese sojourn that I'd end up staying a decade in Beijing, I'd have thought it was highly improbable. As it turned out, I couldn't have planned it better if I had tried!

I feel so fortunate that I was able to witness China's historic transformation firsthand.

My personal transformation was less dramatic, but deeply meaningful nonetheless. Looking back, I can better appreciate the courage and resiliency of a younger me. I grew in my faith and trust, in God and in myself. After my move and in my new role as a consultant, I was able to live much more comfortably, but I am thankful for my experience as a student. My China experienccs alone could fill a book!

Back in the Business World

My move from the university district of Beijing to the Central Business District brought a noticeable shift in my day-to-day life and lifestyle. Consulting suited me; I could largely set my own schedule and maintain my freedom and flexibility, both high on my list of priorities.

My new home was a one-bedroom in a high-rise development just blocks from the heart of the Central Business District, and a short one-stop subway ride. There were four twenty-story buildings forming an arc around a large grassy area. It had the unlikely name of 'Blue Castle' though there was nothing blue about it, but the name sounded good in Chinese.

My landlord was a thirty-something Chinese man who was living and working in Australia. The young woman agent who rented the apartment to me became his property manager, interacting with me when needed, and sometimes just to say "Hi." I felt I was, indirectly, a link for their romance. About a year later they shared with me the happy news they were engaged. I was pleasantly surprised to be invited to their wedding. The occasion was held at a very nice restaurant in a lovely complex with courtyards and pavilions, located at the edge of a park with a lake. I was the only foreigner in attendance and felt quite honored to be included.

My first consulting client was Hill & Knowlton, an international public relations firm. I was brought in to assist in a "pitch," industry vernacular for a formal presentation, for the McDonald's account. During my career I'd worked with several PR agencies, and thus I was familiar with PR work, from the client side. After a few months, a new Managing Director, Esmond, was hired, a Singaporean who spoke fluent Mandarin since most Singapore citizens are bilingual in English and Chinese.

Soon after he arrived, Esmond asked, "Dinah, how would you like to work full time for H&K?"

I was quite surprised and, frankly, I hadn't thought of full-time work.

I replied, "Esmond, I appreciate your asking, but I like being a consultant."

He was not about to take no for an answer. He liked my extensive corporate experience, in both high tech start-ups and Fortune 500 companies, plus my ability to communicate in Chinese. We had a few more discussions and agreed I'd give it a try for six months. I joined the ranks of the other five Directors, all women, reporting directly to Esmond.

I soon found out that one of the big differences between being a consultant and being a Director was that I was now responsible for finding and acquiring new clients. In fact, it seemed winning new accounts became my major job responsibility.

Fortunately, with China's booming economy and the many international companies entering the market or expanding their presence, H&K received a steady flow of Requests for Proposals (RFPs). Depending on industry and workload, these would be assigned to one of the six Directors. I've forgotten the name of the company of my first RFP, but what I do remember is that it was a nerve-racking experience, from beginning to end.

I never learned to like this process, quite the contrary. You suspected that some of the time the company was not serious about hiring an agency, but simply wanted to get some great ideas from the different PR agencies pitching for their business. For this reason you felt reluctant to share your best ideas, yet you needed to make the pitch shine, in hopes of winning the account, just in case.

Happily, my team did win a major new account during my six months. It was part of an international restaurant chain. We worked with them for a very successful launch of their first restaurant in China.

But it was apparent to me early on that, at that stage of my life, full-time employment was not for me. Secondly, the agency business was not for me. I much preferred being on the client side! So H&K and I parted amicably after my six-month contract was finished. Near the end of my six months, my beloved mother passed suddenly. This was a major emotional crisis for me, and I needed time to heal.

Super 8 With Chandeliers

Of the dozen or so clients I worked with over the course of several years, two individuals stand out. They shared some important similarities, though they were very different in terms of age, background, temperament, experience and more.

Both were Caucasian males who had spent half, or more, of their life in China. Both had studied Chinese in their undergraduate days, at a time when very few students did. That, plus their long stay in China had enabled them to be fluent in Chinese. Both were visionaries and pace-setters in their respective industries.

It was a privilege for me to work with them, even though we had our share of frustrating moments.

Mitch was still in his thirties when we first met, at an American Chamber of Commerce luncheon. He had lived and worked in Hong Kong for a number of years, before accepting a position as the Beijing-based Managing Director of a major PR agency. From the start, I sensed his energy; he was always on the move and in a hurry. Within a year he put together a small group of investors and successfully bid to be the China franchisor of Super 8 Motels.

With the country's economic expansion, Mitch saw the need for quality budget motels for the increasing number of local business travelers. They certainly couldn't afford the pricy four or five star hotels, plus these hotels weren't located in the second and third tier cities. And what local hotels there were were invariably poor in quality. In other words, there was a gap that needed to be filled.

Throughout my career I'd been with several start-ups. There's something about the energy of a start-up that appeals to me. There's no road map, thus there's optimal opportunity for creativity and for trying out new things. There's also always a lot more to be done than there are resources available, so everyone has multiple jobs. Challenge and change are two of my favorite words, and you find plenty of both in a start-up.

I remember my first day as a consultant. I took the elevator to the top floor of Mitch's first Super 8 motel, then walked up a flight of stairs. I opened the door and entered a small, very crowded room, which was in a state of chaos. Someone told me Mitch was upstairs. Upstairs? I thought I *was* upstairs. No, I needed to climb, literally, up a small winding flight of steps to another room, equally cramped and crowded. This was where I was to work.

It seemed there were several projects that needed my help, and it was up to me to sort out where to start. Another great thing about start-ups is that no one has the time to tell you what to do. A lot is left up to you to figure out. A key element of success, especially for a start-up, is to hire the right people, people who are self-starters, creative problem solvers who are action-oriented. I knew from the start I would enjoy working with Mitch and his start-up.

The timing was right; there clearly was a market need, but success was far from being a sure bet. For one thing, a couple of larger Chinese economy motel chains had a head start. But Super 8 had a great marketing story to tell, being a foreign brand. And the fact that Mitch could tell the story, in Chinese, to the local media was a boost. The Chinese more readily accept "foreign" to mean better quality, the word carrying a cachet that appealed. Super 8 delivered a superior, more consistent quality, plus a more upscale image, than the local brands.

Many foreign brands, whether fast food chains or other retail stores, invariably upgrade their brand image, as well as their physical premises, when they enter the China market. Some of the Super 8s had marble entrances and enormous crystal chandeliers in the lobby. Not what you'd find in the U.S. for sure. The Chinese owners of these sub-franchises liked the glitz!

My title, Senior Advisor, Marketing was a bit of a misnomer. Yes, I did advise the Founder/President, but invariably I was also the one who did the hands on marketing work, which included creating the Marketing Plan and Budget, writing press releases, writing and creating marketing brochures, flyers, and ads, working with the PR agency, arranging press conferences and, importantly, training the marketing staff.

I could easily have worked forty hours a week, but the budget only called for twenty hours, a conflict and conundrum! Visionary entrepreneurs are usually not very patient, and not the easiest to work for or with. Mitch wisely decided to remove himself from the office and work from his home instead. Staff he needed to meet with would go to his home. This way, both he and his staff got more work done!

Almost from the start, the company and Mitch received industry awards in a number of categories. This all made for great PR and marketing which further enhanced the brand and its growth. A few years ago, Mitch stepped down as the CEO/President. He retains his position as Founder/Chairman, but he's moved on to make his mark in yet another industry.

Mutianyu Schoolhouse at the Great Wall

We were sitting across from each other at a large group dinner. We exchanged the usual, "What do you do?" questions. It was not what he was doing at the time that interested me; it was his vision for the future.

He said, "My wife and I have a weekend house at Mutianyu (part of the Great Wall), and after I retire we plan to live there most of the time."

He went on to say they intended to take over an abandoned schoolhouse and turn it into a restaurant, which would become a tourist destination, with glass blowing, an art gallery, and weekend activities. I was captivated! It all sounded very exciting to me.

A few days later we had a three-hour lunch, together with his wife who he had met when she attended university in the U.S. Jim loved to talk, and I listened intently as he spelled out his vision of being able to provide work for the villagers through an increase in tourism the use of locally grown produce, and implementing environmentally friendly measures in everything they did.

Jim envisioned four different types of restaurants to be located both at Mutianyu and a neighboring village. He needed someone to take all his ideas and produce an integrated Business Plan so he could raise the needed capital from investors. This was something I'd done more than once during my hi-tech start-up days. I agreed to take this on as a consulting project.

Thus I was intimately involved with the birth and the successful launch of the first restaurant, The Schoolhouse at Mutianyu. Mutianyu is one of three well-known sections of the Great Wall. Most of the tourists end up at Badaling Great Wall, the closest to Beijing and the most developed,, which also means it has the most vendors lining the road leading to the Wall. Mutianyu is farther out from Beijing, about a one-and-a-half hour drive. I like it better than Badaling because there's a quaint village at the base of the wall, and it's less crowded.

The first time Jim took me out to see the Schoolhouse, I thought, "Oh, dear!" It had been abandoned for twenty-plus years, and there was only one word to describe it, dilapidated! There were several buildings in the compound, and Jim enthusiastically described the renovation he was going to undertake. The roof of one building was going to be Terrace Dining; it would have a panoramic view of the Great Wall.

Halfway through the Business Plan, Jim could see the contribution I was making, and he wanted me to join full time to head up marketing. Once again, I allowed myself to be swept away by my enthusiasm. Plus, he made me an offer I couldn't refuse—some initial equity in the enterprise. There's an interesting change in relationship dynamics once you go from being a consultant, paid by the hour or by the project, to being an employee, paid a salary. Somehow the clock disappears, and you find yourself putting in much longer hours than expected. What had previously felt like collaboration and consultation now sounded more like demands.

The part of me that values freedom and flexibility, as well as my independence, began to rebel at the constraints and demands, especially after so many years of not answering to a 'boss.' We parted ways cordially, after I implemented all the start-up marketing measures. My last major project was to undertake almost all aspects, including the layout, inside and outside cover copy, editing and proofreading, but not writing the content, of a wonderful little marketing book on the village of Mutianyu at the Great Wall.

.

Stepping Onto the World Stage

Stepping off the plane and into the terminal of Beijing Airport, I saw Olympic banners everywhere. This was September 2000 and the Olympics was being held in Sydney. The 2008 Olympics had not yet been awarded. I was confused. After awhile I realized that, although the colors were the same, the shape of the rings was stylized, more like swirls, just slightly altered. I was fooled by the close facsimile, as I'm sure many people were.

I often think countries take on the characteristics of a person. Studies have shown that having the mindset of a winner helps you to win. By September 2000 when I arrived in Beijing the "Olympic" banners could be seen throughout the city. China adopted the mindset of having already won the 2008 Olympic bid to be the host city before it became a fact. Just like a true Olympic champion.

Over three decades earlier, in 1964, Japan had hosted the first-ever Olympics held in Asia, and twenty-four years later, in 1988, South Korea held its first Olympics. The timing for China to host the 2008 Summer Olympics seemed ideal. But there was a major hurdle. The issue of China's human rights record was a hot topic for debate both within the IOC committee and among academicians, politicians, commentators and the general public.

The two opposing viewpoints were: China should be punished by not awarding it the Olympics because of its record, and others who felt that awarding the Games to China would encourage the government to further reforms. Dr. Henry Kissinger said, "I think it will have a major impact in China, and on the whole, a positive impact, in the sense of giving them a high incentive for moderate conduct both internationally and domestically in the years ahead."

Weeks before the announcement by the IOC of the winning bid, it was the top mind conversation in Beijing, even with the taxi drivers. I've always like Beijing taxi drivers, especially the old hands, those who've been driving for years. They're inquisitive, opinionated, and talkative. More than once I heard, "I hope China doesn't win the bid; the government will need to spend too much money. They should spend the money on the poor areas in China." The dissenters were, of course, in the minority.

As the day drew close for the voting by the IOC Committee, the whole city—indeed, I think the whole country—seemed to be wrapped in an air of anticipation. Beijing was competing against Toronto, Paris, Istanbul, and Osaka, and seemed to be the favorite, especially after its close loss to Sydney eight years earlier.

I was living at the Xijiao Hotel at the time. It was late afternoon on July 13, 2001. There was a knock on my door, and a voice asked, "Dinah, what are you doing?" The door opened; it was a classmate from my Chinese class.

"Studying Chinese as usual," I replied. "You can study tomorrow. Let's go outside to join the crowd and wait for the announcement." There was too much excitement for me to continue studying.

Outside the hotel's front entrance in the circular driveway, a small crowd had gathered in suspense; it felt like we were holding our collective breath. Then the announcement came: Beijing had won the bid on the second round of voting. At long last, China's dream of hosting the Summer Olympics had come true. It was China's turn to step onto the world stage.

****

For the next seven years Beijing looked and felt like one enormous construction site. The construction went far beyond erecting an entire Olympics village with all the venues to hold the many competitions. All of the city's infrastructure was expanded. An enormous new terminal building was added to Beijing airport, with a new subway linking it to the city. Many miles of new subway systems were added, as well as surface roads. New hotels, from five-star to no star, were popping up.

Among my foreign friends, Kelly was the most ardent Olympic enthusiast. In her younger days Kelly had ice skated competitively and remained interested in sports competition.

When tickets for the events became available online, Kelly called me. "Dinah, can you let me have your allocation of tickets if you're not going to use them?"

"Well," I said, "I know I want to attend at least half a dozen, maybe more."

"If you can trust me with your Visa number, I'll draw up an agreement and pay you for the tickets I get plus a discount on the tickets you get."

I'd known Kelly since 2004, when we'd met at the small international church we both attended. She was one of my closest friends, and I knew I could trust her. What I didn't know at the time was that Kelly wasn't just ordering tickets for herself—she was actively engaging in the booming "third party" market for Olympic tickets. She was in contact with entrepreneurs in the U.S. who had clients wanting tickets. Kelly mastered the complex online ordering system and had a profitable summer re-selling tickets. To me, it all sounded too time consuming and complex to bother with.

August 8, 2008 finally arrived. The Chinese have many superstitions about symbols and numbers. The luckiest of all the numbers is "8." As the story goes, it all started in Hong Kong, where the people speak the Cantonese dialect. The Cantonese pronunciation of "8" has a similar sound to the pronunciation of the word for prosperity and wealth. That did it—"8" became the most coveted number. People are willing to pay huge sums to have their phone, license plate, and anything else have the number "8" in it, and it's especially lucky to have a series of numbers end in "8." On the other hand, people shun the number "4" because it sounds like the word for death.

It's no surprise, then, that the date for the opening of the Beijing Olympics was August 8, 2008. Nor should it be a surprise that the Opening Ceremony started precisely at 8:08 p.m. Beijing time. What could be more perfect? 08/08/08 at 8:08!

When I got a call from Kelly, I wasn't surprised. "Dinah," she said," I'm organizing a Peking duck dinner for the 8th before the Opening Ceremony. Some of the people I've been dealing with in the States will be here and they love the idea of Peking duck. The trick is getting a reservation and I'm hoping to get a private room so we don't have to shout to be heard." I told her, "You can count me in Kelly, sounds good."

The truth is, I've never liked Peking duck; I find it too fatty and I once had two pet ducks as a child. Still, it was a festive way to start the evening. Not surprisingly, some of the U.S. visitors got lost trying to find the restaurant, and our dinner was off to a late start. However, the duck was a success and the conversation lively, but there was some anxiety as we were in danger of missing the start of the Opening Ceremony.

Throughout the city there were venues, some indoors, some outdoors, with super-size screens to broadcast the

Opening Ceremony. Getting in was free, but tickets had to be obtained beforehand. We had planned well and had gotten tickets for the screening at the Agricultural Institute, only one subway stop from the restaurant.

As we entered the enormous open hall, the ceremony had already begun ten minutes before. There was no air conditioning and the hall was packed with sweaty bodies; the air was stifling. The large screen was not very sharp, and it was hard to see over the heads of the people in front of the TVs lining the room.

After twenty frustrating minutes I told Kelly, "I'm going home to watch this." I hated to miss part of the ceremony, but I knew there would be re-plays and DVDs.

The Opening Ceremony of the 2008 Olympics was truly an unforgettable event. It's hard to find words to adequately describe this once-in-a-lifetime show of all shows. It was a tour-de-force of creativity and human artistry; it was majestic and magical. As more than one commentator stated, it was a show only China could have produced. It was a magnificent Opening for China's entry onto the world stage.

Looking back, I wish I had attended more events. I think I attended seven in all. Some popular events, like track and field and swimming, were very hard to get tickets for. I ended up going to some less popular events like water polo and beach volleyball, both of which turned out to be a lot of fun to watch. I discovered that some events, like gymnastics, are really better watched on TV for the close-ups, than way up in the bleachers where I was sitting.

Being in Beijing and being able to attend the Beijing Olympics was, undoubtedly, a highlight of my decade in China. It wasn't just the Olympics itself. No, it was much more than that. It was observing the changes that were happening in the society, some subtle, some glaring, in the years leading up to the Olympics. I could feel the increased confidence and pride of the Chinese people, and I could see a city change its skyline and shape, right before my eyes.

China made a most successful debut onto the world stage. A new era had begun.

Her Spirit Left

I think we've all experienced synchronicities in our lives when events or circumstances come together to produce an unexpected outcome, sometimes happy, sometimes not, sometimes both. The story I'm about to share has elements of both.

Since moving to Beijing in September 2000, I'd been fortunate to be able to return to the U.S. once or twice a year to visit family. In one of my life lessons in humility, I learned to accept the financial help my son and my mother gave me to enable me to make these trips home. My son and daughter and grandchildren were on the west coast, and Mom was on the east coast, and I'd divide my time and manage to see some friends as well. I tried to time these trips to include Christmas and/or Chinese New Years.

Starting in 2004, my two sisters, my brother, and I began talking about a big celebration in May 2005 for my mom's 90th birthday. The plan was to have a big family reunion, a weekend of activities. My mom, however, was not excited and did not want a big affair. She'd always been a very private person and seemed to cringe at the idea of being the center of attention for a whole weekend. We couldn't understand her reluctance and simply went forward with our initial plans. At the time I hadn't understood her either, as I now do, reflecting back.

In January 2005, I was visiting Mom. Luckily, I happened to be in her bedroom. She was bending over for something when suddenly her face contorted and she gestured frantically with her hand. I helped her sit on the edge of her bed. She was gasping for air. I wanted to call 911, but she adamantly shook her head and held tightly onto my hand. Somehow, I understood that, in that moment, the most important thing to her was for me to tightly clasp her hand, to not let go to make a phone call. I willed my life energy into her as I prayed, willed her to catch her breath. Slowly, her breath came back. I took her to the emergency room and called her doctor.

She'd had heart problems for a number of years and, for the most part, her medications had kept her situation stabilized. The doctor didn't know what had caused this latest scare. My brother and I were reluctant to leave her alone at the hospital. For the next three days he slept on a cot in her room at night and I arrived in the morning to be with her during the day. At one point while I was in the room, she looked at me and said, with rare emotion, "I have wonderful children."

After returning home and with more rest, Mom seemed her normal self, just a bit more tired. A week later, in a surprising turn of events, my two sisters who lived out of state decided, without prior consultation with each other, to visit Mom. So that weekend in January 2005, all four of us were at Mom's for a happy and serendipitous family get-together. Mom remained uninterested in any discussion about her big birthday celebration.

Sometimes when we siblings were together for more than a day, there could be some discord or disagreement. This time it seemed the weekend was a totally happy one, all of us enjoying being together with each other and with Mom.

The following week, on Sunday, February 6th, I left a note on the kitchen table to let Mom know I was at church.

I often attended this particular church where I'd gotten to know the pastor and where I enjoyed the service. After church I stopped at a bakery on the way home to pick up something I knew Mom liked.

When I entered the kitchen, Mom was on the floor. I immediately called 911, but I knew in my heart it was already too late. Her spirit had left while I was at church.

My heart felt broken. For the first time, I knew what is meant by a broken heart. I had always thought that was simply a metaphor. Now, I knew it was an accurate description of a physically felt pain. I don't know how long the deep and intense pain stayed with me…a very long time. Thankfully time is a healer, and over the months that followed, the physical ache did fade away. I miss her more than words can say. I am grateful she left as she would have wished, quickly and painlessly.

We were all so blessed to have had that one, final, happy weekend with Mom.

Daring To Dream Once Again

I believe that the most important single thing...
is daring to dare.
- Maya Angelou

Time to Return Home

"Jeff, I'm thinking of selling my condo and moving back." I told my son. "My friend Anne just sold hers and got a terrific price." Jeff was taken aback by this sudden news. My decision to return to the U.S. caught my family and friends by surprise. Over the decade I'd been away, I had never talked about moving back. My children had assumed I'd be living in Beijing for some years to come. Given this, they'd generously enabled me to buy a condo a few years earlier. They knew my consulting work ebbed and flowed, and they wanted to make sure I always had a comfortable home.

After my years of putting myself on a strict timetable for breaking the glass ceiling, I'd gone to Beijing purposely wanting to 'go with the flow.' Somehow, I felt I would simply "know" when the time came to return. I had had a health scare, which I never shared with my children as I did not wish to alarm them. Partly as a result of this, I had a growing feeling my health was being adversely affected by the increasing level of pollution in Beijing. And, despite government measures to try and control the amount of traffic within the Beijing metropolitan area, it simply continued to get worse; weekends were as bad as weekdays and peak hour was 24/7.

A good friend of mine, a Chinese American from the States, had bought a condo in Beijing a few months before I did. Anne traveled a few times a year to Beijing to see her parents who had retired there, and for her business projects. We met in Starbucks to catch up.

We'd just sat down with our coffee when she said, "Dinah, I've just sold my condo."

In China, it's perfectly acceptable and very normal to ask the price of things, so I asked, "What did you sell it for?"

When she told me, I couldn't believe it! It was double what she had paid, just a few years earlier. I immediately thought, "Is it time for me to sell?"

In February of 2010, during my visit back to the U.S., I was staying in San Francisco where I'd made plans to get together for dinner with a friend I'd met in Beijing.

Joyce said, "Dinah do you mind if we join some other friends of mine?" I was happy to do so as I always enjoy meeting new people. That's how I met Dave, a retired lawyer living in Chinatown, where he was born.

That same weekend, he asked Joyce to bring me to a neighborhood cafe that had a karaoke bar. He wooed me and wowed me, with his terrific rendition of "San Francisco." It worked, and we began dating.

A month later I had to return to Beijing. We spoke by Skype every day; sometimes he called me twice a day. This continued for several months. It seemed absence was making the heart grow fonder.

My son suspects my decision to move back was prompted by this new relationship. I can't say if that was true on a subconscious level, but I can say it was not, on a conscious level. I sold my Beijing condo, at a nice profit, and moved back to the U.S. in June 2010.

Looking back I do feel rather amazed at myself for simply uprooting from Beijing, which had been home for a decade, and re-locating back to the U.S. without a plan. I have to admit that likely I felt I would be in San Francisco, or nearby, especially given my blossoming new relationship with Dave. But, in the end, San Francisco did not capture my heart. I found it too hilly and too chilly. And it turned out that Dave did not capture my heart either, and the relationship fizzled to a close by year's end.

Close to Dying

Journal - August 2011:
I came close to dying. No, not a physical death. Worse, dying in spirit, in my soul. I was driving one day and, out of nowhere, I burst into tears and sobbed so hard I could barely drive. My heart hurt, physically. Deep within me, I knew why I was sobbing. I was slowly letting my dream die. I had long dreamed of being an author, of being a speaker, yet I was doing nothing to pursue this dream. I had let myself be lulled into living a comfortable enough life, coasting into retirement. Yet I knew I could not let my dream die. I could not die with my song unsung. I still had much to give, to offer, to the world. I had not fully utilized all my God-given talents.

From that moment on, and in the months that followed, I'd read what I've written above and renew my determination to follow my dream, no matter what!

Rescuing My Dream

Soon after this, I serendipitously received an email from someone I'd never heard of, Rick Frishman, offering his 'Author 101' three-day conference at the Westin, Los

Angeles airport. I immediately signed up, just before the deadline for the early discount. It was a packed three days, filled with speakers and panels talking about all aspects of becoming and being an author. I was blown away by all the great information and very surprised at the integral role of social media in all this.

Brendon Burchard, another person I'd never heard of, showed up in my inbox,. I bought his book, *The Millionaire Messenger*, and signed up for his weekend seminar, Experts Academy, in September. I was impressed by this young man, full of energy and exuding charisma. He reminded me of a digital-age, more intellectual version of Tony Robbins whose seminars I had attended twenty-five years earlier. Two months later I signed up for another of his seminars, then a conference. Three Brendon Burchard events in a row! Even for a workshop junkie like me, that's a record.

As if I hadn't had my fill of wonderful workshops, in December of 2011, I happened upon a free webinar hosted by Amy Ahlers, Christine Arylo, and Sophia McCloud. I'd only briefly heard of Amy and Christine. At first, I was a bit put off by the title of the workshop they were offering— "The Great Work." Who me? Called on to do my great work in the world? I was both inspired and intimidated by the idea and vision. I listened to the hour-long webinar and what they said captivated me. I was intrigued enough to apply for the seven-month program. Marketing genius— have people apply for a nearly five figure program! Despite the very hefty fee, the most I'd ever paid at that point for any program, I signed up.

I believe in divine serendipity—the perfect book, workshop or webinar bringing us just what we need, often before we even know we need it. The program launched in January 2012 with a weekend retreat in beautiful wine country, just north of Napa. There were twelve of us, from all over the country. It was a magical weekend as we were led into soulful meditation, contemplation, ceremony, and creative exercises. We also set our intentions for the seven months. My intention was to finally start writing my book. 2012 was off to a great start!

Returning to Freedom

Journal, February 2012
" I was a free spirit as a child—outgoing, talkative, popular, an exceptional student and always self motivated to be the best!

After marriage, I started to feel restricted, constrained, 'toned down'—to be more in the background (to my ambitious husband), seen but not heard. In fact, the handwriting was on the wall before I got married, and I almost broke off our engagement, but my left brain won out and I relented.

DARING TO DREAM ONCE AGAIN

I remember feeling as if I would burst if I did not set myself free. For years, I could not take a full deep breath; my breath would literally stop midway. I saw some doctors, but there was nothing they could do, and I reconciled myself to this condition. Even ten years after my divorce it was still this way. I can't remember when I was finally healed, finally able to breathe fully.

After my MBA from Columbia in 1980, during my climbing-the-corporate-ladder years, I felt free, not letting myself be constrained by the corporate world.

My decade in Beijing I felt free, to follow my heart's desire and do as I wished.

It was upon returning to the U.S. in 2010 that I began to have a sense of "shoulds." I should settle down in one place, I should find something that could both occupy my time and make some spending money, I should enjoy a quiet retirement.

A sense of terror enveloped me. It seemed a life of quiet desperation was facing me. I found my spirit again shouting out to be set free—free to dance, free to explore, free to soar to heights unknown, free to dream once again.

And so, in December, 2011, with my 70th birthday looming, I made the decision to join a tribe of Great Women, led by three

Great Leaders, to receive the support and love to create my Great Work!"

Dark Night of the Soul

Sometimes, just when things are looking great, Spirit throws us a curveball, or that's what if feels like. In my case, it was a fastball that I didn't see coming, and it hit me hard. Seemingly overnight, what had, over the years, been an amicable and even warm relationship with my son-in-law turned chilly soon after my move back from Beijing. After a year, I found an ideal new apartment, and it never even occurred to me to discuss this beforehand with him and my daughter. Alas, being less than ten minutes away from them turned out to be "too close for comfort" and things really took a nose dive. There were other reasons, though I may never know what they are.

The unhappy result was a greatly reduced access to my two grandchildren who were so dear to me. I missed them so much. My heart ached not to be with them, to play and laugh with them. I became obsessed with not being able to see them more than every other week for dim sum lunch. It was on my mind non-stop, and I felt increasingly sad and despondent. My life energy slowly seeped out of me. I couldn't sleep and I could barely function to carry out daily chores. I didn't even have the energy to talk above a whisper.

My doctor at the time ran the usual tests. At our appointment, she said, "All your blood work came back normal; you're fine." But I certainly didn't feel fine. Her attitude indicated she'd done her job. I decided to take matters into my own hands, as we all must, when it's our own health. I went to see a homeopathic practitioner who ran some tests and told me I had adrenal burnout. My own guess is that this could have started during my high stress years climbing the corporate ladder. I'd always had high energy, but low stamina, getting tired very easily.

After six weeks of changes in my diet and a slew of herbal supplements, I felt only slightly better. I went to a Chinese doctor for a series of acupuncture treatments, three times a week, for six weeks. Again, not much improvement. Finally, I went to a chiropractor, Dr. Mary Reimer. Prior to this I'd only gone to a chiropractor twice in my life. Frankly, it scared me more than seeing a dentist. But Dr. Mary had such a comforting and caring approach, and she gave the best healing hugs.

In the meantime, our GreatWork seven-month program was cruising along. Of course I expected myself to keep up with the work, despite my weak and unwell condition. As my energy continued downhill it became more and more of a struggle for me to focus, to even start, let alone finish anything. I fell increasingly behind. My website and other projects were not getting done. My anxiety attacks became worse and more frequent. I was on a downward spiral. Sometimes I felt my body literally shaking. I tried EFT (emotional freedom technique) without noticeable effect. I believe EFT can and has helped thousands and maybe I just needed more guidance and patience.

Finally, by June, in my weekly call with my 'accountability partner,' I told her, through my tears, "Kate, I simply don't have the energy to make our final retreat in July. It tires me to even whisper. I don't think I can make the two-and-a-half hour drive." I asked Kate to pass my message on.

The next day Amy called and, in the gentlest, most caring tone, she said, "Dinah, you can attend as much, or as little, of the sessions as you feel able. You can rest or lie down on the sofa in the back. Please come; we just want your presence with us."

After we hung up, I had a new resolve to be there. I couldn't talk above a whisper, but I could give and receive hugs. Do you know how healing hugs can be? It felt right to be there, our circle of twelve women who had shared this wonderful seven-month journey.

Reflection: *It was a valuable lesson for me to decide to attend and be OK showing up in my weakened state, with my voice only a whisper and with my projects unfinished. The erstwhile star student didn't get an A for work completed, but I gave myself an A+ for just being there, for showing up. It was a personal victory!*

What I thought was going to be a terrific year had turned out to be a year of challenges and learning. It made me stronger, both physically and emotionally. I made changes in my diet and found a new caring doctor. Most importantly, I learned lessons in self-compassion, self-love and self-acceptance. Spirit gifted me with 'growing pains' and I grew.

15 Minutes a Day Magic

As 2013 began, my book was still in my head, not on paper. I had long lists of chapter and sub-chapter titles. What I didn't have was actual prose. I found myself mulling over, endlessly, my chapter and sub-chapter titles. What I now know is that a subconscious part of me was having a hard time accepting that my book was not to be a 'self help' book with personal stories as examples. Instead, it would be a memoir, with 'life lessons.'

A voice repeated, "Who are you to write a memoir? Who would read it, who would care?"

I finally told myself, "It doesn't matter if no one cares, except me. I care." I wanted, and needed, to put my story on paper, for my grandchildren and their children. I wanted them to know, even a little, about their "Oma" and great-grandparents and appreciate their good fortune in growing up in America.

I've long believed that just the right book, seminar or webinar comes along when we need it. Samantha Bennett (Sam) came onto my computer screen offering her course "Get It Done!" Just what I needed. A big incentive for me to sign up for her three-month online course was the weekend retreat, "The Big YES!" in San Diego. If you haven't guessed by now, I love all kinds of retreats, seminars, workshops. The energy of being with like-minded and like-hearted people is such a boon to the spirit!

A belief I've always had about seminars and workshops is that if I learn just one thing helpful to my personal or professional development, then it's worth my time and money. What I got from Sam is that YES, I can spend at least fifteen minutes a day writing my book. And this has to take priority before anything else, especially email. Sam pounded these two points home.

Old habits die hard. Many times, as I was about to start my day, I'd stop and ask myself, "Dinah, can you spend just fifteen minutes on your writing right now?" Sometimes, I'd have to dialogue about this with myself, debating if I could spend fifteen minutes. This all sounds ridiculous, I know. After all, writing my book was a deep desire and something I dearly wanted to do.

I don't think I'm alone in this, however. How many of you have something you deeply desire to do, produce, or create but somehow you never get started? Your dream gets lost in your "to do" lists.

One reason I hadn't started, besides the confusion over my myriad chapter and sub-chapter titles, was my belief I needed a block of time, at least an hour, before I could get started. Guess what? I never got started. The secret is to just get started! Sounds like that Nike ad! Of course once I got started, it was never just fifteen minutes. It somehow stretched to thirty, sixty, or even ninety or more minutes.

Reflection: *It seems paradoxical that which is most profound—be they words, practices or scientific formulae—is simple. We like to make things complex, and we tend to equate complexity with value. Actually, the opposite is true.*

Transformational Author

I was lying on the veranda at my son's house, enjoying the peaceful and beautiful view of a small valley. The water falling into the small pool sounded soothing and melodic in the stillness. I had my laptop, and for some reason decided to listen to a tele-seminar by Christine Kloser. Near the end of the hour-long session, she invited listeners to her event in September, less than a month away. Christine is known as the Transformation Catalyst and has helped thousands of authors to birth their books. I felt a tug to sign up.

Thus it was I found myself attending Christine's Transformational Authors Breakthrough event in Baltimore, MD, along with a hundred other attendees. I didn't know what to expect from this three-day event, but somehow I sensed it would be different. The first day, Christine stood at the door of a darkened, candle-lit room, and personally gave each of us a big welcoming hug, all one hundred of us. Now I knew it would be different!

In her opening remarks she said, "There are some of you here who have no idea why you are here, but you simply felt you needed to be here." How very true, and I was one of them. For three days Christine had the stage mostly to herself, with no notes, simply speaking from her heart and taking us into small group exercises as she felt the energetic needs of the room. She created a sacred space and transformation happened. As she states, "My events are a true co-creation with the people in attendance."

At the end of the event, nearly two dozen of us signed up for her high-end nine-month MasterHeart (note, not Master Mind) program. The core of this program was to collectively birth a new book, "Pebbles in the Pond Wave 3: Transforming the World One Person at a Time." Each of us wrote a chapter for this third edition of the book, which was published in June, 2014.

As part of the program, Christine hosted a three-day retreat after all the chapters were submitted. Some couldn't make it, but there were sixteen who could, women from the U.S., Canada, Thailand, Germany, and Greece, a wonderfully diverse group. The only man in the room was Christine's husband, who helped as needed but also sat in circle with us as we engaged in our exercises and sharing. Somewhat remarkably, he fit right in and his presence added to the group. Again, Christine created the sacred space and transformations happened. The experience we had cannot be described; it could only be felt by being there.

Christine helps authors write books that are transformative on four levels: first, for the author, second, for the reader, third, for your business, and lastly, for the world. How does this happen? We were led through a process to excavate deeply within our souls for our 'Why' before we began. And we constantly remind ourselves of our 'Why' whenever we need motivation to continue. Am I always able do this? Unfortunately not. But I continue trying.

Reflection: *If someone were to ask me what lessons I've learned in my seven plus decades, I could come up with a long list. But if I were asked for the single most important lesson, it would be a very short answer: Listen to your heart. I've come to believe this is the overarching lesson I've learned over the years, and continue to learn. The decisions which brought me the most joy and fulfillment were made listening to my heart, and the ones which did not turn out so happily were made listening to my head. Nonetheless, I have no regrets, because I believe, in the* *bigger scheme, there are no mistakes—only lessons to be learned. It's a process, a process of learning to trust that still, small voice within that whispers the truth to us."The truth shall set you free."*

Writing this book has, indeed, been a transformational journey. It has given me pleasure and pain. It has brought me 'Ah ha!' moments of insight into myself. It has brought me to tears, tears of joy and tears of sadness. No tears of regret, however. I believe that everything and every person who comes into our life comes for a reason, and brings a gift, though sometimes the gift is wrapped in sandpaper, as Lisa Nichols would say. Time and again we hear of how a person's worst moment or experience turned out to be the best, and I do believe this.

I wrote this book to fulfill a deeply and long held desire and dream of mine. *Daring to Dream Once Again* is, first and foremost, a challenge to myself.

It is also a challenge to you, dear reader. It is my deep desire for you to follow your dream, wherever it may lead you, and to tell yourself 'It's never too late!'

What a privilege and opportunity to share my stories and life lessons with you. My deepest thanks and gratitude to you for taking this journey with me. May you always continue to dare to dream once again!

A Mother's Wish For Her Daughter

I would like to end my story, and this book, where I began it—with my mom. Mom always took great care in choosing the cards she sent. She'd take her time reading card after card at the Hallmark store, looking for just the right words and the perfect card. Sometimes when I was with her I'd feel a bit impatient and wish she'd hurry up.

Out of the dozens of cards I received from Mom over the years, there was one that was particularly special, and I put it separately into a file folder. I came across it while writing this book. It touches my heart deeply and brings tears of sadness and joy. It's a testament to how wise she was—and how well she knew me. For some reason she didn't put a date on it, as she usually did. Perhaps she did this consciously—the words and sentiment are timeless, and I treasure them, as I treasure her memory.

HOW TO MAKE
A Beautiful Life
Reflections For A Daughter
On Her Birthday

Love yourself.

MAKE PEACE with who you are

and where you are

at this moment in time.

Listen to your heart.

If you can't hear what it's saying

in this noisy world,

MAKE TIME for yourself.

Enjoy your own company.

Let your mind wander among the stars.

Dear Dinah,
Happy Birthday

Try.

Take chances.

MAKE MISTAKES.

Life can be messy

and confusing at times,

but it's also full of surprises.

The next rock in your path

might be a stepping-stone.

Be happy.

When you don't have what you want,

want what you have.

MAKE DO.

That's a well-kept secret of contentment.

Love Mom

There aren't any shortcuts to tomorrow.
You have to MAKE YOUR OWN WAY.
To know where you're going
is only part of it.
You need to know where you've been, too.
And if you ever get lost, don't worry.
The people who love you will find you.
Count on it.

Life isn't days and years.
It's what you do with time
and with all the goodness and grace
that's inside you.
MAKE A BEAUTIFUL LIFE...
The kind of life you deserve.

About the Author

Dinah Lin is a Chinese American author and inspirational speaker in the "Fifth Stage" of her life. This stage began on the cusp of her seventieth birthday after she returned from living for a decade in Beijing. She is living her latest dream by sharing her message "It's never too late."

Before moving to Beijing, Dinah spent over 25 years as a senior executive in high-tech start-ups and Fortune 500 companies. She also spent three-and-a-half years as a senior political appointee in the George H. W. Bush administration in Washington, D.C.

Born in Shanghai, Dinah escaped with her mom and two siblings on the last boat leaving the city in 1949. Raised in Ohio, she later lived for fifteen years as a young wife and mother in Hong Kong, Singapore, Malaysia, Thailand, and the Philippines. This experience greatly deepened and expanded her appreciation and understanding of Asian culture.

Dinah has always felt immensely proud of her double heritage. Her dream is being a bridge of understanding between America and China, and inspiring others to dare to dream once again.

She received her BA in economics from Barnard College and her MBA from Columbia University. She now resides in California near her son, daughter, and three grandchildren.

Connect with Dinah at www.thedinahlin.com

Made in the USA
Columbia, SC
02 January 2018